AF351262

CHARLIE MILLER

The Vanishing Verdict Series: Book 3 of 7

Samira, Ethan & Jonas Crime Thriller Series 3

Copyright © 2025 by Charlie Miller

All rights reserved. No part of this publication may be reproduced, stored or transmitted in any form or by any means, electronic, mechanical, photocopying, recording, scanning, or otherwise without written permission from the publisher. It is illegal to copy this book, post it to a website, or distribute it by any other means without permission.

This novel is entirely a work of fiction. The names, characters and incidents portrayed in it are the work of the author's imagination. Any resemblance to actual persons, living or dead, events or localities is entirely coincidental.

Charlie Miller asserts the moral right to be identified as the author of this work.

Charlie Miller has no responsibility for the persistence or accuracy of URLs for external or third-party Internet Websites referred to in this publication and does not guarantee that any content on such Websites is, or will remain, accurate or appropriate.

Designations used by companies to distinguish their products are often claimed as trademarks. All brand names and product names used in this book and on its cover are trade names, service marks, trademarks and registered trademarks of their respective owners. The publishers and the book are not associated with any product or vendor mentioned in this book. None of the companies referenced within the book have endorsed the book.

First edition

This book was professionally typeset on Reedsy.
Find out more at reedsy.com

Contents

Prologue

Prologue:

Jonas Hale stood in the courtroom, the heavy weight of his briefcase in his hand, his eyes trained on the jury. It was supposed to be the defining moment of his career—the point where he would present the evidence that would clear his client's name and prove his innocence beyond a shadow of a doubt. He had spent months gathering it all: security footage, alibi testimonies, the solid chain of events that would dismantle the prosecution's case piece by piece. Today, it was all supposed to come together.

The case was simple, or at least, it should have been. Damien Thorpe, a man wrongly accused of the brutal murder of his business partner, had an airtight alibi. Jonas had reviewed every detail, every piece of evidence, and had spent hours preparing his argument, sure of one thing: the truth would win. But now, as he stepped into the courtroom, a sudden unease gripped him, tightening in his chest.

He glanced at the judge, whose expression seemed detached, as if everything that was about to unfold didn't matter at all. The jury sat silently, their faces expressionless, waiting for the case to begin.

Jonas took a deep breath, feeling the weight of every eye in the room on him. This was his moment. He would present his evidence, tear down the flimsy case the prosecution had built, and prove Thorpe's innocence. He was ready. He had to be.

But when he opened his briefcase and reached for the first document—the surveillance footage that clearly showed his client's alibi—his fingers froze.

The file wasn't there.

Jonas quickly flipped through the papers, his heart beginning to race. The file that had been so carefully prepared, saved and printed in his office just the night before—gone. He felt his pulse quicken, a bead of sweat forming at his brow. He turned to look at the evidence box, where the thumb drive containing the footage should have been.

Nothing.

His stomach twisted as a sickening thought crept into his mind. This couldn't be happening.

"Mr. Hale," the judge's voice cut through his panic, his tone neutral but firm. "Are you prepared to present your evidence?"

Jonas swallowed hard, forcing a nod. He was prepared—he had to be. "Yes, Your Honor. I—just a moment." He turned back to the table, searching frantically, but the footage was gone. His mind was racing. There had to be an explanation. There had to be.

He tried to push the panic down, but it was growing, clawing at the edges of his thoughts. He had been so meticulous, so careful. How could this be happening?

His eyes flicked to the prosecutor's table, and there, standing with an air of practiced indifference, was the opposing attorney, Richard Lang. Lang met his gaze with a faint, almost knowing smile, as if he'd been waiting for this very moment. Jonas quickly looked away, his stomach churning. Was Lang involved in this? Was this a deliberate attempt to sabotage his case?

"Mr. Hale?" the judge repeated, his patience wearing thin.

Jonas straightened his back, forcing himself to focus. "Yes, Your Honor. I—" He stopped, his eyes scanning the room. There had to be another way to prove his client's innocence. He had other evidence, other witnesses. The alibi was rock solid. He could still make his case. But when he looked down at the documents for the witness testimony, his blood ran cold.

The names were there, but the details were missing. The addresses were blank. The statements had been erased. Every shred of the alibi he'd planned to present had evaporated.

A sharp, quiet gasp came from the back of the courtroom, and Jonas turned to see one of the jurors glancing nervously around, as if something had just occurred to them. They knew it too—something was wrong, terribly wrong.

He felt a cold sweat trickling down his neck. How could this be happening? His mind raced, but no answers came. The prosecution seemed to be playing along, their behavior so unnervingly calm, almost as if they knew the case was rigged— but were afraid to speak out. It was as though the entire system had been carefully manipulated, from the evidence to the very people in the room.

"Your Honor," Jonas said, his voice unsteady, "I must request a brief recess."

The judge stared at him, his gaze unreadable. After a long pause, the judge nodded curtly. "Recess granted. We will reconvene in thirty minutes."

Jonas exhaled, his mind spinning. He walked briskly out of the courtroom, ignoring the eyes that followed him, and made his way to the hallway. His hands were shaking, his grip tight on his briefcase as if he could hold onto some shred of reality by holding onto it.

He couldn't think straight. Something was happening, something beyond his control, and he had no idea how to stop it.

His phone buzzed in his pocket, a message from Samira Cross. He pulled it out, hoping for some clarity, some connection to the outside world. Samira had been the only one to believe him when he'd first brought up the strange, unsettling shifts in reality that had been plaguing his life for weeks.

"Jonas, we need to meet. This is bigger than we thought. You're not just fighting for your client's life—you're fighting for your own existence."

A cold shiver ran down his spine as he read the message, the implication hanging heavily in the air. He hit reply quickly.

"I'll meet you. Now."

Samira and Ethan had been his lifeline in the past, but now? Now, Jonas wasn't sure who to trust. The more he pieced together the strange occurrences surrounding his cases, the more it seemed that someone—or something—was erasing the truth, erasing people, erasing history itself.

He couldn't let this happen—not to his client, not to himself. If the truth was disappearing before his eyes, how could he possibly stop it?

Jonas rushed out of the courthouse, his mind racing. He had no more time to waste. He had to find out who was pulling the strings and how they were erasing his life, one piece at a time.

But as he looked up, his eyes widening in horror, the ground beneath him seemed to shift. The courthouse—everything—began to blur, as if the world itself were unraveling at the seams. He was being erased.

And the truth was slipping away with him.

One

The Unlikely Client

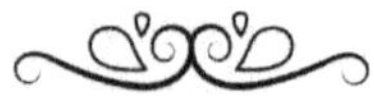

Jonas Hale sat at his polished mahogany desk, the late afternoon sun casting long shadows across the room. His office, perched high in one of Eridale's sleek corporate towers, was an epitome of order. The bookshelves were neatly arranged, the file cabinets stacked with the weight of cases long past, and in the corner, an antique lamp flickered dimly, adding an air of quiet contemplation. But today, the sterile calm that usually comforted him felt distant. His hands were shaking.

The file sitting in front of him was thick, filled with evidence—evidence that was almost too compelling. He could already see the damning points: the bloodied crime scene photos, the witness testimonies, the matching DNA. But still, something didn't sit right. He could feel it in his gut, that quiet discomfort that, as a defense attorney, he had learned to trust.

Damien Thorpe. The name was unfamiliar. The man had been accused of murdering Vera Novak, a successful executive at a tech company—Voryx Technologies—whose body had been discovered in a high-end apartment in the city. The case had been publicized across every news outlet, and the evidence seemed to speak for itself. It was a case made for a guilty verdict. But there was one problem.

Damien Thorpe insisted he was innocent.

Jonas skimmed through the case summary. Thorpe had been arrested immediately after the murder, his fingerprints found on the murder weapon. Several witnesses had seen him leave the building that night. The prosecution had a strong case, and everything pointed toward Thorpe as the murderer. Still, Damien clung to his innocence, his desperation oozing from the defense statements Jonas had read earlier.

Something felt wrong. It wasn't just the evidence, but the context. The case was too perfect, too neat. A man with everything to lose, caught in a web of lies. But why? And why was Damien's insistence on innocence so adamant, so unsettling?

Jonas leaned back in his chair, staring at the case file. It had arrived on his desk just this morning, a new case from a law firm he had worked with on occasion. They had asked him to take it on—insisted, actually. There was something about the way they had presented it that didn't add up. Jonas was good at reading people, and this felt like a game. But what was the angle? Who was playing whom?

He shuffled through the pages and paused at the victim's background. Vera Novak had been a rising star at Voryx Technologies, a cutting-edge AI company that was rapidly becoming one of the most influential players in the tech industry. The firm was known for developing state-of-the-art software capable of everything from automating business decisions to tracking vast amounts of personal data. But the more Jonas read, the more he felt the walls closing in. There was more to this woman's life than just her tech achievements. There were darker connections, and the closer Jonas looked, the murkier the picture became.

Voryx Technologies. The name had lingered in the back of his mind, faintly at first. He knew it had been involved in several controversial legal battles before—privacy breaches, a few shareholder disputes, even allegations of corruption. But nothing that had stuck. Still, Jonas couldn't shake the thought that this company was somehow at the heart of it all.

His phone buzzed on the desk, interrupting his thoughts. It was an encrypted message from Samira Cross, a journalist he had worked with on a few cases in the past. Samira had a knack for uncovering things people didn't want to be found, and she was one of the few people Jonas trusted in a world full of unreliable sources.

He opened the message.

"Jonas, I've got something on the Vera Novak case. Voryx Technologies isn't just a passive player here—they're too involved. I need to talk to you. This goes deeper than what you're seeing on the surface."

Jonas' pulse quickened. Samira had a way of cutting to the chase, but this felt different. It wasn't just another story she had uncovered—it was a warning. Something about this case was worse than anyone realized.

He quickly dialed her number. The phone rang three times before Samira's familiar voice picked up.

"Jonas," she said, her tone clipped but urgent. "I've been looking into Vera Novak's past. You need to understand—Voryx Technologies has some serious skeletons in their closet. I've found some connections to Damien Thorpe that don't match up with the narrative you're getting from the cops and the media."

"I figured something was off," Jonas replied, rubbing his temple as he flipped through the rest of the file. "Everything points to Thorpe, but he keeps insisting he's innocent. I don't buy it, but—"

"Listen to me," Samira cut in. "Vera Novak wasn't just an employee at Voryx. She was involved in some deep-level dealings with the company's higher-ups. I've been tracking down her emails, and I found references to a side project— something about manipulating data streams. I think Voryx was using her to cover up something much bigger than a simple murder."

Jonas paused, looking at the page that listed the victim's ties to Voryx Technologies. "What do you mean by manipulating data streams? You think it's connected to the case?"

"I think it's everything. I don't have all the details, but I've tracked the project she was working on—it involves a proprietary system of altering personal data records. I've seen something like this before. Jonas, this is connected to what's going on with Thorpe. The murder wasn't random—it was targeted. Someone's pulling the strings."

Jonas leaned back in his chair, a creeping feeling of dread washing over him. "Samira, I don't have time for cryptic answers. Are you saying Thorpe didn't kill her? That someone at Voryx did?"

"Not exactly," Samira said, her voice tight with urgency. "But something about the entire case feels staged. Vera's murder, Thorpe's arrest—this isn't just about a woman and her tech company. This is about rewriting history, erasing people's existence, and manipulating memories. And I think Voryx is at the center of it all."

Jonas stared at the phone, his thoughts racing. He had been hired to defend a man accused of a brutal murder, but now the case had turned into something far more complex, something that touched on forces he didn't understand. What if Samira was right? What if this wasn't a simple murder at all? What if the very system he was trying to protect—the justice system, the law—was part of the deception?

"I need to meet you, Samira. Tonight," Jonas said, his voice resolute. "I'll take this case, but I need you to dig deeper into Voryx. I need everything you have."

"Got it. I'll be in touch soon," Samira replied, hanging up.

Jonas sat back in his chair, staring at the open file before him. Everything had changed in a moment. His task was no longer just about saving a man's life. It was about uncovering a far-reaching conspiracy that could tear apart everything he knew. He was standing on the precipice of something massive, and there was no turning back.

Damien Thorpe's trial had barely begun, but Jonas could already feel the weight of the storm that was coming. And the deeper he dug into Voryx Technologies' ties to the case, the more dangerous things were becoming. If Samira's hunch was right, then this was no ordinary murder—it was a case that could unravel the very fabric of society.

Two

The Vanishing Evidence

Jonas Hale sat in the dimly lit corner of his office, the papers spread out before him like a puzzle he was struggling to piece together. The desk was cluttered with pages of Damien Thorpe's defense, with witness testimonies, crime scene photographs, and forensic reports—each more damning than the last. But something didn't feel right. No matter how many times he reviewed the material, he couldn't shake the sense that there was something lurking beneath the surface, something he wasn't seeing.

Damien Thorpe had insisted he was innocent from the beginning. His claims were vehement, but Jonas, like everyone else, had been swayed by the overwhelming evidence against him. After all, how could someone—especially a man with so much to lose—deny something so clear-cut?

But as Jonas continued to dig into the case, he started to notice inconsistencies. Minor details that didn't match, witnesses whose statements seemed… off. The murder victim, Vera Novak, had been found in her luxurious apartment with signs of a brutal attack. The police had already placed Thorpe at the scene, and the victim's blood was found on his clothes. The evidence seemed airtight. But as Jonas sifted through the case files, something gnawed at him. The more he investigated, the more elusive the truth became.

He glanced at the clock. Late. Hours had passed since he'd started reviewing the material, and his mind was growing weary. But something was wrong. He could feel it.

Jonas reached for the file containing the evidence of Vera Novak's connection to Voryx Technologies. A tech giant based in Eridale, Voryx had been at the center of several high-profile controversies, but its involvement in Novak's life was nothing short of troubling. The more Jonas delved into the company's affairs, the more questions arose. But as he began to cross-reference the data, it began to slip from his grasp.

He opened the first file with the intention of cross-checking Novak's involvement with Voryx, but the document was gone. No, not gone. It had been altered. The words on the page shifted, and entire paragraphs disappeared in front of his eyes, leaving him staring at an empty sheet of paper. His hand froze over the page, and he blinked, willing his vision to focus.

"What the hell?" Jonas muttered under his breath. His head began to pound, and a tightness crept up his neck as he turned the file over. He shuffled through the remaining pages of the file, hoping the rest hadn't been tampered with. But every piece of evidence he had collected—every statement, every detail—was gone, replaced by blank sheets of paper. His pulse quickened. Something was wrong.

He dialed the number for his assistant, Olivia Pierce, his

fingers trembling as he tried to control his mounting frustration. She answered after the first ring.

"Jonas, what's going on?" Olivia's voice was steady, but there was an edge of concern.

"I need you to check the security footage," Jonas replied, trying to steady his breathing. "The footage from the night of the murder. I need it on my desk in the next hour."

Olivia hesitated. "I'll get right on it, but… Jonas, is everything okay? You sound off."

"It's fine. Just make sure the footage is real." His voice was sharper than he intended, but he didn't have time to explain. He couldn't explain.

He hung up the phone and leaned back in his chair, rubbing his temples. The case had gone from strange to bizarre, and now it was slipping into the realm of impossible. How could this happen? How could everything—every piece of evidence, every lead—vanish as if it had never existed?

The door to his office creaked open, and Jonas snapped his head up, startled. Standing in the doorway was Samira Cross, her eyes scanning the room before she stepped inside. She had a look of urgency in her eyes, as if she already knew what was going on. She was one of the few people Jonas trusted, a journalist who always seemed to know when something was wrong, even before the rest of the world figured it out.

"Samira," Jonas said, his voice strained. "You shouldn't be here. This case… it's getting weird. I can't explain it, but I think something's happening. Someone's erasing everything."

Samira raised an eyebrow, her curiosity piqued. "What are you talking about? What's disappearing?"

Jonas pushed the files across his desk in frustration. "Every-thing. Documents. Witness statements. Evidence. It's as if someone is intentionally erasing it all, one piece at a time. I don't know how it's happening or why, but I'm starting to think that the people behind this are much more powerful than I imagined."

Samira walked over and picked up one of the blank files. She flipped it open and frowned. "This doesn't make sense."

Jonas nodded grimly. "No. It doesn't. And that's not all. I've been looking into Voryx Technologies—the company Novak was involved with. There's something strange there. Connections, hidden ties to people we don't even know."

"Voryx Technologies?" Samira repeated, her expression shifting to one of deep thought. "I've heard rumors. You know, whispers in the industry. They've been linked to some pretty shady dealings."

Jonas leaned forward, clasping his hands together. "That's what I'm afraid of. But I can't prove anything yet. And now, the case has just… disappeared."

Samira set the file down. "Jonas, this doesn't feel like a coincidence anymore. You're onto something bigger than just a murder case."

Jonas looked up, meeting Samira's gaze. "I think you're right. But the more I dig, the more I realize that someone is controlling the narrative—rewriting the past, erasing history. It's like… it's like none of this was meant to happen in the first place."

A chill ran through him as he spoke, the weight of his words settling over them both. Samira was quiet for a moment, processing what he had said. Then she nodded.

"I can help," she said. "I've been looking into Voryx too. I'll see what I can find."

Before Jonas could respond, his phone buzzed with an incoming message. He glanced down, and his heart skipped a beat. It was from Olivia.

"Jonas, the footage is gone. It was never recorded. It's as if it never happened."

Jonas dropped the phone on his desk, feeling the walls close in. His worst fears were coming true. This was no longer just a missing piece of evidence or a fabricated story. This was an orchestrated effort to erase the truth, to manipulate everything.

Samira's voice broke through his thoughts. "We have to get ahead of this. We need to find out who's behind it and why."

Jonas exhaled slowly, trying to calm his racing mind. "But how? How do we even begin to fight something we can't see?"

Samira's eyes glinted with determination. "By doing what we do best. By digging deeper. We're not alone in this, Jonas. You've got me. And you've got Ethan. We'll find out what's really going on."

Jonas nodded, a surge of renewed purpose flowing through him. They didn't have all the answers, but together, they could start pulling the threads. They would unravel the mystery—and expose the people pulling the strings.

As the sun set outside the window, casting the room in shadows, Jonas knew one thing for certain: he was no longer just fighting for his client's life. He was fighting for the truth—whatever it took, and whatever it cost.

Three

The Missing Witness

Jonas Hale stood outside the courthouse, a cool breeze ruffling the papers in his hand. His mind was spinning, each thought a jagged puzzle piece he couldn't seem to fit together. The case against Damien Thorpe had been riddled with holes from the start, but every step he took only made the problem deeper. His client, a man insisting on his innocence, was sitting in a cell, with mounting evidence that painted him as the cold-blooded murderer. And Jonas… Jonas had never been more convinced of a man's innocence, yet everything in the case screamed otherwise.

Today was supposed to be the turning point. A key witness, someone who had been in the vicinity of the crime scene, had contacted Jonas with crucial information. This witness was the last hope in turning the tide of the trial in Damien's favor. But now, as Jonas stared at the courthouse doors, a gnawing sense of dread curled in his stomach. He was about to meet the witness, and somehow, he could already feel something was wrong.

Inside, the courthouse was its usual hectic self—lawyers pacing the halls, whispers floating between the rows of benches, and the shuffle of paper filling the air. But to Jonas, it all felt hollow. He had seen this all too many times before: a system that failed to serve justice, a system more interested in protecting its own than ensuring the right people were held accountable.

He pulled himself together and walked into the witness room, where he was supposed to meet his key player in the case. As he opened the door, he expected to see the witness, someone by the name of Carla Hollingsworth, sitting there with her nervous eyes and unsteady breath. But when Jonas entered, there was no one. The room was empty.

Confused, he stepped further into the room, glancing around. The air was still, unsettlingly so. The chair where the witness should've been sitting was empty. Her coat, the one she'd worn when she'd met with him a few days prior, was gone. No sign of anyone having been there. It was as though she had evaporated into thin air.

"Carla?" Jonas called, his voice tentative, as though somehow expecting her to appear from behind the curtain or from some other corner of the room.

But there was no response.

His pulse quickened, and he instinctively reached for his phone. He dialed the number Carla had given him, waiting as the line rang. The phone's steady tone echoed in his ear, but the call went unanswered. Frustrated, Jonas tried again, but still nothing. He paced the room, his eyes scanning the corners, the windows, the door. Nothing.

Minutes passed before he left the room, his frustration mounting. The hall outside was as busy as ever. He walked up to the clerk's desk and asked for any information about Carla Hollingsworth's whereabouts. The clerk, a young woman with a tired smile, looked up from her work with a faint sense of confusion.

"I'm sorry, sir, but there's no record of a Carla Hollingsworth being scheduled for any testimony today, or at all," she said, raising her eyebrows as if the name was unfamiliar.

Jonas' confusion deepened. "No record? But I spoke with her just a few days ago. She contacted me. She was supposed to testify in the case. She's a crucial witness."

The clerk's face remained blank. "I'm afraid there's no mention of her in the system. Are you sure you have the name right?"

Jonas felt a chill run through him. He leaned forward, trying to keep his voice steady. "I'm certain. This woman contacted me directly. I've met with her. Her testimony could change everything for my client."

The clerk hesitated, then typed something into her computer. She paused, frowning. "I'm sorry, sir, but there's no trace of this person anywhere in the system. It's as if she's never existed."

A cold dread settled over Jonas like a heavy fog. His mind raced, turning over possibilities, but none of them made sense. Could someone have erased her from the records? Was this part of the larger conspiracy he'd been unknowingly drawn into?

He left the clerk's desk without saying another word, his heart pounding as he walked out into the courtyard. His mind swirled with a thousand questions, but none of them brought clarity. He couldn't help but wonder—what if this wasn't just an isolated incident? What if it was a deliberate act? A move to keep him from uncovering the truth? If they could erase a witness, what else could they erase?

His phone buzzed in his pocket, pulling him from his thoughts. He pulled it out and saw Samira's name on the screen.

"Jonas, where the hell are you? I've been trying to reach you," Samira's voice was sharp but filled with urgency.

"I'm at the courthouse. Something's wrong. The witness—Carla Hollingsworth—she's gone. No trace of her. No record. It's as if she never existed," Jonas explained quickly, his voice low as he tried to calm himself. "I don't know what's going on, but I'm starting to think this case is bigger than I thought."

"Damien Thorpe? Bigger? You're not wrong. But this isn't about him. Listen carefully, Jonas. I've been digging into Voryx Technologies. Their connections to the murder victim, Vera Novak, aren't just business-related. There's something darker, deeper. I think Voryx is involved in more than we know."

Jonas' eyes widened. "You've got to be kidding me. I've been following the Voryx lead. What did you find?"

"I think Voryx has been controlling events behind the scenes. Manipulating the truth. And Carla Hollingsworth… she was connected to them. I'm not sure how, but I have a lead on some internal documents. They're buried, but I think they'll lead us to the people orchestrating all of this. Stay put. I'm on my way."

Jonas ended the call and sank down onto a nearby bench, the weight of everything pressing down on him. Was it possible that Voryx Technologies was behind this? That they had the power to manipulate not just the case, but entire lives? He had already suspected the company had its hands in something shady, but this was beginning to feel like something much larger than he had ever imagined.

The sound of a car engine revving in the distance pulled him from his thoughts. He stood up, his eyes scanning the area. He didn't have time to waste. He had to get to the bottom of this.

Moments later, Samira's car pulled up to the curb. She got out, her face tight with determination. "You're not going to like what I've uncovered," she said, walking up to him quickly. "Voryx is involved in erasing people from the record. The company's been at the center of several high-profile disappearances—people who have been erased from history. Carla was likely one of them."

Jonas took a deep breath, running a hand through his hair. "What do we do now?"

"We keep digging. We find out who's pulling the strings. And we do whatever it takes to expose them." Samira's eyes flashed with resolve. "But first, we need to find out what happened to Carla Hollingsworth. And why she's been erased."

Jonas nodded. The stakes had just gotten higher. He had thought he was simply defending an innocent man. Now, it seemed like the case was much bigger than he ever could have imagined.

As he followed Samira into the car, Jonas couldn't shake the feeling that he was walking into a storm—one that would tear apart everything he thought he knew about justice and the law.

And as they drove away from the courthouse, Jonas couldn't help but wonder: How many more lives had been erased? How much of the truth had been buried? And most chilling of all, who was next?

Four

A Shadow in the Court

The courtroom was filled with the usual hum of whispered conversations, the rhythmic rustling of legal documents, and the soft clink of the gavel. But for Jonas Hale, it all felt like an illusion. The weight of his new case, the vanishing evidence, the mysterious disappearance of Carla Hollingsworth, and Samira's troubling lead about Voryx Technologies—it was all starting to unravel in ways he couldn't have anticipated. The legal system he had spent his life defending, with its rituals, its rules, its expectations, was beginning to show cracks. And Jonas was standing right at the edge of it.

He glanced at Damien Thorpe, his client, who sat silently beside him in the defense booth, his eyes hollow with desperation. The man's fate hung in the balance, yet the more Jonas dug into the case, the less sure he was of what he was even fighting for. The evidence—damning in its simplicity—painted Damien as the murderer. But something felt deeply wrong. No matter how much Jonas tried to push forward, every step felt like it led to a dead end.

As the trial progressed, Jonas found himself revisiting old notes, re-reading witness statements, and wondering if the answers he was looking for were being deliberately kept from him. The whispers of something larger, a shadowy hand manipulating the system, started to feel like more than just paranoia.

It was during one of these restless nights that Jonas received an unexpected call. The voice on the other end was low, distorted, and tinged with urgency.

"If you want the truth, meet me at the courthouse in one hour. Bring no one with you."

Before Jonas could respond, the line went dead. The message was simple, and it rattled him to his core. What was going on? Who was this person? And why the courthouse?

There was only one thing left to do. He grabbed his coat and made his way to the courthouse, his heart pounding with a mixture of anticipation and dread. Was he being drawn deeper into something he couldn't control?

He arrived at the courthouse, its towering facade now casting a long shadow over him. The courtrooms were quiet, closed off for the night, but a single light still burned in one of the hallways. The door at the end of the corridor was slightly ajar, and Jonas pushed it open without hesitation.

Inside stood a figure cloaked in shadow. The dim light revealed little of the person's face, but Jonas could make out the sharp lines of a suit, the hint of a tie beneath the high collar. The person's presence felt like a force of nature—intense, calculating, and ominous.

"You came," the voice said, not a question, but a statement of fact. It was calm, controlled, and carried an unsettling weight.

"I don't know why I'm here. Who are you?" Jonas asked, trying to steady his voice, but there was a tremor he couldn't hide.

The figure smiled, though it was more of a subtle curl of the lips than a true gesture of warmth. "I don't expect you to understand. You've been digging for the wrong things, Jonas. That's why you haven't found anything."

Jonas stiffened, the words landing like a blow. "What are you talking about?"

The figure stepped closer, and the faint light revealed more of their features—sharp, angular, with an unsettling calm that seemed almost otherworldly. "I'm here to offer you something that could save you from making a very big mistake. You think this case is just about Damien Thorpe, don't you? That it's about clearing his name."

Jonas said nothing. He wasn't sure what to say. He could feel the weight of the situation bearing down on him.

"This is not just about a man's life, Jonas. This is about a system that is being manipulated—erased—by powers you can't begin to comprehend. Powers that don't just control the courts; they control reality itself. The Revisionists."

The words hit Jonas like a bolt of lightning, and for a moment, he froze. His mind raced, but he struggled to connect the dots. "The Revisionists?" he repeated, his voice barely audible. "What the hell is that?"

The figure's smile deepened. "An organization with one goal: to rewrite history. To erase inconvenient truths, manipulate the past, and control the narrative. The courts are just one piece of the puzzle. But there's a much larger game at play. You've seen the signs. The disappearing evidence, the missing witnesses, the strange manipulation of records. All of it leads back to them."

Jonas swallowed hard, his mouth dry. He could feel his pulse quickening. "This is insane. You're telling me there's a secret society running the courts? That they're behind this whole case?"

The figure nodded slowly, almost pityingly. "Not just this case. Many others. The trial you're defending is merely a distraction, a carefully orchestrated play to hide what's really happening behind the scenes. Voryx Technologies? They're tangled in this too. The victim in your case, Vera Novak, had connections to them. But it's bigger than just one company."

Jonas felt his head spin. Everything he thought he knew about justice, about the law, seemed to be crumbling before him. His entire career was based on defending the system, but what if the system was broken beyond repair? What if the very institutions he had trusted had been hijacked by forces he couldn't see?

"You're not crazy, Jonas," the figure said, as if reading his mind. "Everything you've uncovered is real. But you're not going to find the answers you're looking for by following the paper trail. You're chasing shadows."

The figure paused, allowing the words to sink in. "The Revisionists are watching. They know you're getting closer to the truth, and they'll stop at nothing to erase you, just like they've erased the others."

Jonas's mind raced. "What do you want from me?"

The figure took a deep breath, the air in the room thick with tension. "You have two choices. You can keep fighting this case, blindly, hoping you'll find the truth in the darkness. Or you can join us, and we'll show you the way. You'll never get the answers you need on your own, Jonas. You're not the first to come this far, but you might be the last to survive it."

Jonas's heart hammered in his chest. He felt trapped in a nightmare, his world spinning out of control. Everything he thought he understood about the law and justice had been turned upside down. The Revisionists, this shadowy organization, had infiltrated the very heart of the legal system. And Jonas, whether he liked it or not, was caught in the middle.

The figure stepped back, melting into the shadows once more. "You'll find us when you're ready. Just know that you're not alone. And if you choose to fight, be prepared. The truth is dangerous. It's not something you can simply uncover. You'll have to fight for it."

With that, the figure was gone, leaving Jonas standing alone in the quiet, dimly lit hallway. The weight of their words hung in the air, and for the first time in his career, Jonas felt a deep, unsettling fear—not for his client, but for himself.

The case had taken a turn into something much darker than he had anticipated, and the shadow of The Revisionists loomed over him, threatening to consume everything he had ever believed in. The walls were closing in.

Five

The Tipping Point

J onas Hale sat behind the defense table, the weight of his legal pads pressing against his palms, a faint sheen of sweat starting to form on his brow. The courtroom seemed colder than usual, the hum of the fluorescent lights overhead echoing in his ears as he shifted his focus between the judge's bench and the prosecution's table. Damien Thorpe, his client, sat beside him, a hollow figure whose eyes were hollow with despair, his lips tight with the unsaid words that could shatter everything. Jonas's mind was far from his client. It was elsewhere—wrestling with a growing sense of dread. How could a case go so wrong? Why was everything he had uncovered slipping through his fingers like sand?

The case had never been straightforward. When Jonas first agreed to take on Damien's defense, he believed in the man's innocence—or at least, he hoped to find a crack in the system that would exonerate him. But as the trial went on, that hope dissolved, replaced by a gnawing suspicion that someone or something was blocking his every move. There had been a series of strange disappearances. Not just evidence, but people. Witnesses had vanished, security footage had been erased, and more than once, Jonas had found himself facing dead ends, as if someone had been working against him the entire time.

The judge, an older man whose face was creased with age and responsibility, slammed his gavel on the desk. The proceedings had ground to a halt in a way that was almost too deliberate, as though every movement was meticulously timed. Jonas's mind flitted between thoughts, his fingers gripping the edge of his papers, and he couldn't shake the cold, prickling sensation in the pit of his stomach.

"Mr. Hale, if you're not ready to present the next witness, I'm going to have to issue a ruling."

Jonas blinked, startled from his thoughts. He had been so absorbed in his mounting desperation that he hadn't realized the trial was continuing. His thoughts moved too fast, one after the other, as the prosecution smirked across the room, utterly unfazed by his disarray.

"I'm ready, Your Honor." Jonas forced his voice out, trying to conceal the tremor that edged his words.

The judge nodded, waiting for him to proceed. A glimmer of doubt clouded Jonas's resolve, but he knew that he had to keep pushing. Even if the entire system felt rigged against him, there was no turning back. He had to fight for Damien, for justice, or whatever was left of it.

Jonas stood and walked to the witness stand, glancing over the files before him. The document, the one piece of evidence that could have turned the tide in his favor, was gone. He had just reviewed it an hour ago—this exact moment in the trial.

But now it was missing, vanished into the ether, as if it had never existed. Panic clawed at him.

"Your Honor, I will be calling a witness to the stand, but I must inform the court that the necessary documents—" Jonas's voice faltered as the courtroom seemed to shrink around him. He felt as if the walls themselves were closing in, constricting his every breath.

Across the room, the prosecution's attorney, a smooth and self-assured man named Lawrence Bell, adjusted his glasses and raised a brow. "Your Honor, it seems Mr. Hale is having trouble presenting his case. Perhaps he has no case to present at all."

Jonas looked toward the judge, whose expression had hardened into one of indifference, or was it something else? He couldn't tell. The atmosphere in the courtroom was suddenly oppressive, as if something invisible, something malevolent, was hanging over everyone's heads.

"I have no further questions, Your Honor," Bell said in a cool tone, clearly satisfied with his attempt to disrupt Jonas's momentum. "I trust the defense has concluded its presentation?"

The words hung in the air like a challenge.

Jonas's heart raced. He wasn't ready for this. He needed more time to find the evidence, to confirm his theories, to confront what was really happening. But as he glanced at the jurors, their faces were blank slates, unreadable. Some of them seemed to be glancing at each other, sharing subtle glances, almost as if they were in on something Jonas wasn't privy to. A shiver ran down his spine, and his grip tightened on the edge of the podium.

"Your Honor, I request a brief recess," Jonas said, forcing his voice to steady. He could feel the weight of the court's gaze on him, the oppressive silence as everyone waited for the judge's decision.

The judge hesitated, then nodded. "Ten minutes."

As the courtroom emptied, Jonas found himself alone, his mind racing. He grabbed his briefcase and walked quickly out of the courtroom, his breath coming faster with every step. He needed answers—something, anything—to explain what was happening to him, to his case. As he stepped into the hallway, he pulled out his phone and dialed Samira Cross's number.

"Jonas?" Samira's voice was brisk, but there was an undercurrent of worry. "What's going on? Is Damien still going to get a fair trial?"

"I don't know anymore, Samira," Jonas said, his voice low. "Something's wrong. I've been chasing this case, trying to expose the truth, and it's all slipping away. I can't find the evidence, the witnesses are disappearing, and the prosecution— there's something strange about them. It feels like they're playing along with it, like they know something I don't. I think I'm up against something bigger than I imagined."

There was a brief pause before Samira responded, her voice steady and filled with determination. "What if this is more than just a messed-up trial, Jonas? What if you're dealing with something much more dangerous—something that's manipulating the entire legal system?"

Jonas stopped in his tracks. Her words hit him like a sledgehammer, an ugly truth that he hadn't fully allowed himself to acknowledge. He had suspected it, of course—the strange disappearances, the way the evidence was vanishing, the eerie way the prosecution had been behaving. But now, hearing Samira say it out loud, it clicked.

"Samira, what if you're right?" Jonas muttered, rubbing a hand over his face. "What if this isn't just a case? What if there's something—some force—erasing the truth right in front of me? And if it's powerful enough to do that, what happens if it starts erasing me, too?"

"You need to keep going, Jonas. You're not alone in this. I've been looking into something. Voryx Technologies. It's a shady tech company connected to the victim, Vera Novak. They've been tied to some unusual dealings in the past, and I think they're hiding something—something that might be directly linked to this trial. I'll send you everything I have. You need to dig deeper into their involvement."

Jonas felt a surge of hope as he realized Samira was still pushing forward, uncovering the pieces he couldn't. But he also knew that the deeper he dug into this case, the more dangerous it was becoming. What if the people behind this— The Revisionists, as Samira had suggested—were not just manipulating this case, but every case they touched?

"What happens if I can't stop this, Samira?" Jonas asked, his voice barely above a whisper.

"You stop them, Jonas. You expose them for what they are. You find the truth, no matter how far down the rabbit hole it takes you. You're in this too deep to turn back now."

Jonas's jaw clenched as he stared down at his phone, the weight of Samira's words sinking in. He wasn't going to let this go—not now, not when the stakes had grown so high.

He was going to fight. But the question was, could he even trust the very system he had spent his career defending?

As the sound of footsteps echoed down the hallway, Jonas knew that whatever happened next, the game had changed. And there was no turning back.

The truth was out there. He just had to survive long enough to uncover it.

Six

The Vanishing Client

Jonas sat in his office, staring at the stack of case files in front of him. The paperwork was beginning to blur together—documents, notes, police reports—all of it seemed to melt into a chaotic mess. But the real chaos was in his mind. The trial had begun, and the walls were closing in faster than he could keep up with.

Damien Thorpe, the man Jonas had been defending for the past few weeks, was becoming more and more unpredictable. What started as a case that felt like it could be a routine wrongful conviction was now unraveling in ways that made Jonas question everything.

It wasn't just the missing evidence or the unexplained disappearances anymore—there was something deeper at play. The more Jonas interacted with Damien, the more the man's behavior raised alarms. He had seen the change in his client's demeanor before, but now it was glaring. Damien's once calm, almost stoic nature had shifted into something darker. His eyes darted around the room with an almost paranoid intensity, his hand shaking when he spoke, and his posture rigid as if he were trying to hold himself together.

At first, Jonas thought it was just stress. After all, facing a life sentence for a crime he didn't commit would make anyone anxious. But the more Jonas observed, the more he realized that Damien's paranoia was growing. It wasn't just about the trial anymore. It was as if Damien was afraid of something—or someone—outside of the courtroom.

Jonas had tried to reason with him. "Damien, you need to calm down. This isn't helping your case. We need you focused, not nervous."

But the man had barely looked at him. His eyes were fixed on the door, as if he expected someone to walk in at any moment.

"I can't trust anyone, Jonas. Not anymore. They're watching. I know it. I'm not crazy," Damien whispered, leaning closer, his voice low and shaking. "You have to believe me. I don't know who they are, but they're everywhere. They've been following me."

Jonas felt the hairs on the back of his neck prickle. Damien had been insistent for days now, and Jonas had tried to dismiss it as stress, as a man on the edge, but there was something about the way Damien said it that made Jonas uneasy.

"I'm here to help, Damien," Jonas said, trying to keep his tone steady, but doubt was creeping in, crawling up his spine. "But you need to focus on the facts. We've got to stick to the evidence."

Damien's eyes were wide now, frantic. "The facts? The facts are all wrong. All of them. It's not real, Jonas. It's all been staged. They've manipulated everything. The trial, the witnesses, the police reports. You have to listen to me. You can't trust anything anymore. They're controlling everything."

Jonas sat back in his chair, his stomach tightening. He had seen paranoia before, but something about Damien's words felt different—more desperate. And it was starting to creep into Jonas's own mind. Was it possible? Was he being played? Was Damien truly innocent, or was he part of a much larger game?

Jonas had seen things before that couldn't be explained. The missing evidence, the erased records, the disappearing witnesses. But Damien's behavior was different. It wasn't just the case that felt off anymore. It was everything. The walls of the courthouse, the halls of the police station—they all felt like part of the illusion. Was he the one being played, or was it Damien?

Jonas needed answers, and fast. He couldn't let this case slip through his fingers. If Damien was lying, it would be the end of everything. But if he wasn't—if there was something bigger going on—Jonas had to find out what it was before it was too late.

Later that afternoon, Jonas drove to the courthouse, his mind still reeling. He'd left Damien at the detention center with instructions to stay calm. But something told him that things weren't going to stay calm for long.

As Jonas walked into the courtroom, he noticed a few familiar faces: the prosecutor, Lawrence Bell, who had been annoyingly smug throughout the trial, and the judge, who had an air of indifference to the entire process. But what caught Jonas's eye were the two men sitting in the back of the courtroom, staring at him. They didn't look like the usual spectators or journalists. Their eyes were too intense, too focused.

Jonas's gut tightened. They were watching him. He tried to

ignore them, but their gaze followed him every step of the way. He could feel the heat of their stare on the back of his neck as he took his seat at the defense table.

The trial proceeded, but Jonas couldn't shake the feeling that something was wrong. The case, the trial—it felt like a setup. Everything was too neat, too perfect. Every move he made seemed to be countered with some unexpected turn, a piece of evidence that disappeared, a witness who didn't show up.

But then something happened that shifted the entire course of the day. As Jonas was reviewing the police records again, something caught his eye. A discrepancy. A missing date, a file marked "confidential" that hadn't been flagged before. The records seemed manipulated, altered. They didn't just vanish— they had been rewritten, as though someone had gone back in time and changed them.

Jonas's heart pounded in his chest as he realized the implications. This wasn't just a random act of corruption. This was something much more calculated. Someone was controlling the trial, controlling the evidence, controlling the very fabric of justice.

Before he could process what this meant, his phone buzzed in his pocket. It was Samira Cross. He quickly answered the call, trying to mask the growing panic in his voice.

"Jonas, I've found something," Samira's voice crackled through the line, her tone urgent. "Voryx Technologies. They're connected to the case. But it's not just about Vera Novak. It's bigger than that. They've been involved in manipulating evidence, controlling information. They're part of something much larger."

Jonas's breath caught in his throat. Voryx Technologies. He'd heard the name before, but it had always been a distant thought, an afterthought. He never imagined it would be tied to Damien's case. But now, it was all starting to come together.

"Samira, are you sure?" Jonas asked, his voice hoarse. He glanced at the prosecutor, who was busy talking to the judge, and then back at the two men in the back of the courtroom.

"I'm certain. I'm sending you the files now. But you need to be careful, Jonas. Something isn't right. They've been watching us," Samira warned.

Jonas glanced at the door of the courtroom, then back at the files in front of him. There was no time to waste. He had to act fast.

"Thanks, Samira. I'll look into it," he said, hanging up the phone. But as he tried to focus on the case again, the two men in the back stood up, their eyes locked on him. One of them gave a small nod, and then they both turned and walked out of the courtroom.

Jonas's pulse quickened. His instinct screamed at him to follow them, but he stayed seated. If these men were connected to the case, if they were involved in the conspiracy, then Jonas knew one thing for sure: the real fight had only just begun.

Damien's case wasn't just about a wrongful conviction anymore. It was a battle against an unseen enemy, an enemy with the power to rewrite history itself. And Jonas was right in the middle of it.

Seven

Collapsing Walls

The walls of Jonas Hale's office were closing in on him. He had always been the type to take control of his cases—he was known for his meticulous attention to detail, his unyielding dedication to justice, his ability to get to the truth no matter how ugly or convoluted it might be. But now, every answer he uncovered seemed to unravel everything he thought he knew. Every step forward only seemed to drag him deeper into a nightmare where reality itself was being rewritten.

Jonas sat at his desk, surrounded by piles of case files, trying to make sense of the chaos. The documents in front of him no longer felt like solid evidence. They felt like ghostly fragments of a reality that was slipping through his fingers. Every word on the page seemed to blur, and the more he tried to focus, the more disoriented he became. He rubbed his temples, trying to fight the pounding headache that had become a constant companion in recent days. The trial was falling apart, and so was everything else in his life.

Damien Thorpe's case was only the tip of the iceberg. What had started as a routine defense had spiraled into a nightmare. The more Jonas dug, the more the walls between his world and an unknown, sinister force began to crack. Evidence was vanishing, witnesses were disappearing, and now… now, it was his own life that seemed to be eroding.

He picked up the phone, staring at the screen. The name was familiar, but the memory of the person attached to it wasn't. It was his old colleague, Detective Michael Graves. They had worked together for years, investigating some of the city's most complex cases. They'd spent countless hours side by side, fighting for justice. But now, when Jonas dialed his number, the voice on the other end of the line was strange, unfamiliar.

"Detective Graves," Jonas said, trying to sound confident, though his voice wavered. "It's Jonas Hale, we worked together—"

"I'm sorry," the voice cut in, "but I don't know you. Who did you say you were?"

Jonas's stomach sank. The line went silent for a moment, and then the voice on the other end spoke again, this time with cold detachment.

"You've got the wrong number, I think. I don't know anyone by that name."

Jonas stared at the phone in his hand, his mind racing. This had to be some sort of mistake. Maybe Graves had left the department, maybe he had a new number. But deep down, Jonas knew something was wrong. How could Graves not know him? They had been colleagues for years.

He hung up and tried again. This time, he reached someone

who had once been his close friend—a former law school classmate, Anna Porter. The conversation started off like it always did, with polite pleasantries and small talk. But then, as the conversation progressed, something shifted.

Anna's voice wavered, almost as if she was struggling to place him.

"I'm sorry, Jonas, I… I don't remember. We met in law school, right?" she asked, but there was hesitation in her voice.

Jonas's mind began to race. "Anna, it's me, Jonas Hale. We studied together, we worked on cases together."

The line went quiet, and for a moment, Jonas thought she had hung up. But then, her voice returned, cold and distant.

"I don't know you. Maybe you have the wrong number. I don't think I've ever met anyone by that name."

Jonas dropped the phone into his lap, his hands trembling. His world, once so solid and grounded in the law, in people he trusted, was now unraveling. His colleagues, his friends—they were all beginning to vanish from his life. But how? Why?

He felt the walls of his office closing in on him, the air thick and suffocating. The room felt smaller, the corners more oppressive. He tried to focus on the case—on Damien Thorpe, on the disappearing evidence, on the growing presence of the Revisionists, but it was hard. Everything was slipping through his fingers.

The door to his office opened, and his assistant, Michelle, stepped in, holding a stack of paperwork. She didn't even look at him as she set the papers down on his desk.

"Everything alright, Mr. Hale?" she asked, her tone neutral, almost too neutral.

Jonas stared at her. There was something in the way she spoke that made his skin crawl. She had always been kind, professional, but now, she seemed like a stranger. There was no warmth in her voice. No recognition.

"Michelle, do you… do you remember me?" Jonas asked, his voice hoarse, his throat tight.

She paused, blinking at him for a moment, and then smiled faintly, but there was no warmth in it. It was just an empty gesture.

"Of course I do, Mr. Hale. You're my boss. Is everything okay? You've been a little… off lately."

Jonas rubbed his eyes, trying to gather his thoughts. "Michelle… we've worked together for years. You've been with me through all of this. You know who I am."

Her smile faded for just a fraction of a second before it returned. "I know who you are, Mr. Hale. You're my boss, and you've been working hard on the case. Is that what you mean?"

Jonas couldn't stop the cold shiver that ran down his spine. Was this a coincidence? Was he imagining things? Why did everything feel so wrong?

"No," he said softly, shaking his head. "No, it's not just the case. Something's wrong. It's like… like everyone's forgetting me. Like I'm… fading."

Michelle's expression remained the same, but there was something strange in her eyes. A flicker of something, maybe pity, maybe confusion. But it was gone as quickly as it had come. "Mr. Hale, you should really take a break. Maybe get some rest. I'll handle things for now."

Jonas stood up abruptly, knocking his chair back. "I need to speak to someone who remembers me. I need to find out what's happening."

But Michelle just stared at him, an unreadable expression on her face.

"Mr. Hale," she said slowly, "You've been working yourself too hard. Maybe you need to leave the office for a while. Take some time off."

Her voice was calm, soothing, but Jonas felt like it was a sedative—a soft way to shut him down.

"I can't leave. Not now. Not when I'm this close to understanding what's happening," Jonas replied fiercely, his voice tinged with desperation.

Michelle didn't respond. Instead, she turned and left the office, closing the door softly behind her. Jonas stood there for a long time, the silence pressing down on him.

Suddenly, his phone buzzed again, jerking him out of his thoughts. It was an email—a simple message from an unknown address:

"You've been forgotten. It's too late."

Jonas stared at the screen, his mind spinning. What did it mean? Who was it from? And why did it feel like the walls were closing in tighter around him with each passing second?

In that moment, he realized the truth: his world was no longer his own. Someone—or something—was erasing him from it. From the case, from the memories of those he had known, and even from the very fabric of reality itself.

Jonas Hale was becoming a ghost in his own life.

Eight

Unseen Manipulation

The weight of the case was suffocating. Jonas Hale had always prided himself on his ability to unravel the most complex legal puzzles, but the deeper he dug into the mysteries surrounding Damien Thorpe's trial, the less certain he became. His once firm belief in the law, in the fairness of the justice system, was starting to feel like a distant memory. The fabric of his reality was unraveling, and with it, the very concept of justice itself.

Jonas sat in his office late into the night, a bottle of scotch half-empty beside him. His desk was littered with papers, each one leading him further into a labyrinth of confusion and despair. He rubbed his eyes, exhaustion weighing heavily on him, but he couldn't stop. There was too much at stake. The case, Damien's innocence, and his own sanity were all tangled together in a mess he couldn't ignore.

He had just finished reviewing another batch of evidence—if

you could even call it that. Witness statements, security footage, even the most basic documents had all been corrupted or erased. A simple phone call to the courthouse revealed that files related to the case had vanished without a trace. But that wasn't what unsettled him most. No, it was the mounting feeling that someone, or something, was orchestrating all of this.

A soft knock on the door interrupted his thoughts, and Jonas glanced up. Samira Cross stood in the doorway, her presence a welcome break from the isolation that had consumed him. She had been helping him piece together the puzzle, but even she seemed on edge these days, her once confident demeanor replaced by a wariness that mirrored his own.

"Jonas, we need to talk," Samira said, stepping inside and closing the door behind her.

Jonas nodded, motioning to the chair across from him. "I'm listening. I've been digging into this case until my eyes are bleeding, but I'm not getting anywhere. Are you finding anything useful?"

She hesitated, her eyes flicking to the papers scattered across the desk. "Actually, yes. I've been looking into Voryx Technologies. And I think I've found something… unsettling."

The mention of Voryx Technologies made Jonas stiffen. He had seen the company's name appear in the case files multiple times, always in connection with Vera Novak, the murder victim. Novak had been involved in a high-profile tech venture before her untimely death, and her ties to Voryx raised a red flag. But he hadn't had the time to follow up—until now.

"Voryx?" Jonas repeated, leaning forward in his chair. "What did you find?"

Samira took a deep breath. "It's worse than we thought. Voryx Technologies isn't just a shady tech company. They have ties to some of the most powerful figures in the legal world. I've found evidence that suggests they've been manipulating the justice system for years."

Jonas's stomach dropped. "Manipulating the system? How?"

"I'm not entirely sure yet, but from what I've gathered, Voryx has access to technology that can rewrite not just records, but entire histories. I'm talking about erasing people, changing events, altering perceptions of reality itself. It's like a dark web of corruption, and Voryx is at the center of it."

Jonas's mind raced. "That's… that's impossible. No one has that kind of power."

"Apparently, they do," Samira said, her voice grim. "And it's not just about erasing people. It's about controlling the narrative. Controlling the truth."

Jonas stared at her, the pieces starting to click into place. He had been thinking about this case all wrong. At first, he had believed that the disappearances, the missing evidence, the strange behavior of his colleagues and friends, were isolated incidents. But now, he realized that there was something much larger at play—an organized effort to control not just the legal system, but reality itself.

"So, what are they trying to do? What's their endgame?" Jonas asked, his voice barely above a whisper.

Samira shook her head. "I don't know. But I'm starting to think that Damien Thorpe isn't just a pawn in all of this—he's a part of a much bigger scheme. A scheme that goes beyond just one man's wrongful conviction. It's about power, control, and the rewriting of history."

Jonas stood up, pacing across the room, his thoughts spinning. He had always been a man of logic, of facts. But now, everything he knew was being shattered. He had to figure out who was behind this—and fast. If Voryx Technologies was involved, then this wasn't just about Damien's case anymore. This was about exposing a conspiracy that could change the very nature of justice.

"I need to find out more," Jonas said, stopping in front of his desk. "If Voryx is really behind this, I need proof. I can't just walk into court and claim that a tech company is controlling everything. I need something concrete, something I can present."

Samira nodded. "I agree. But be careful. I've been digging into Voryx's employees, and some of them have… disappeared. People who were working on projects related to their AI technology have gone missing without a trace. It's like they never existed."

A chill ran down Jonas's spine. The more he learned, the more the whole situation began to feel like a nightmare. The Revisionists, the disappearances, Voryx Technologies—it was all starting to connect in ways that didn't make sense, but also made too much sense.

"I'll be careful," Jonas said, though he knew the danger had already found him. "I have to keep digging. If this is true, then we're not just dealing with a corrupt case. We're dealing with an entity that can manipulate time, history, and truth itself."

Samira's eyes darkened. "And that's the problem. If someone has the power to erase history, then no one will ever know what really happened. It's the perfect crime."

Jonas glanced at the clock on the wall. It was getting late, and the exhaustion was starting to weigh on him. But he couldn't stop now. Not when he was so close. He had to find the source of this power. He had to uncover the truth.

"I'll need your help," Jonas said, turning to Samira. "If we're going to take down Voryx and The Revisionists, we can't do it alone. We need to stick together."

Samira smiled, a small but reassuring gesture. "You're not alone, Jonas. We'll get to the bottom of this. We have to."

As she left the office, Jonas felt the weight of the case settle back onto his shoulders. The pieces were falling into place, but the picture they formed was a terrifying one. He had no idea how deep the conspiracy went, or who might be behind it, but he knew one thing for sure: there was no going back now.

The Revisionists had already rewritten too much. If Jonas didn't stop them, they would rewrite everything.

The next morning, Jonas began making calls to sources he had been avoiding. He needed answers, and he needed them fast. He had no idea where to start looking for Voryx's dark secrets, but he was determined to find out.

As he worked, a knock at the door interrupted his thoughts. Jonas looked up, surprised to see a courier standing in the doorway. The man held out a sealed envelope, and Jonas took it with a furrowed brow.

The courier left without saying a word, and Jonas ripped open the envelope, finding a single sheet of paper inside. The message was simple, written in an elegant but anonymous hand:

"You're getting too close. Stop now, or we'll erase you next."

Jonas felt the blood drain from his face as the implications hit him. The game had changed. He wasn't just fighting for a client anymore. He was fighting for his own life.

Nine

The Disappearing Act

Jonas Hale walked through the hallways of the law firm, his footsteps echoing in the quiet space. The building, once bustling with energy, now felt like a mausoleum. The air felt thick, oppressive, as though something unseen was slowly suffocating everything in its path. He had to find someone—someone who could help him make sense of all this. Someone who could confirm the things he was beginning to suspect.

His office had been useless. No matter how many documents he pored over, they just seemed to slip through his fingers, as if they were being erased, one by one. The case with Damien Thorpe was a lost cause—every shred of evidence that might have exonerated the man had vanished. Witnesses, crucial testimony, even the security footage from the night of the murder had all been altered or completely erased. But it wasn't just the case that was falling apart—it was everything around him.

He had tried reaching out to one of his most trusted colleagues, Daniel Webb. They had worked together on dozens of cases over the years. But when Jonas called him last night, he had received a strange response. Daniel's voice, normally warm and familiar, had been cold, distant. When Jonas had mentioned the case they had been working on, Daniel's response was simple: "I don't know what you're talking about."

It didn't make sense. They had been close—partners in the truest sense of the word. Daniel had always been there, his sharp legal mind guiding them both through the toughest cases. But now, it was as if the man didn't even remember their years of collaboration.

Jonas stood in front of Daniel's office, his hand hovering over the doorknob. He was nervous, though he wasn't sure why. Maybe it was because he already knew what he was about to face. Maybe it was because he could feel the walls closing in, a pressure in his chest that he couldn't shake.

He opened the door and stepped inside.

Daniel's office was just as he remembered it—neatly arranged, stacks of files on the desk, a few legal books neatly lined up on a shelf. It looked like nothing had changed, but the man sitting behind the desk was a stranger.

"Jonas!" Daniel greeted him with a smile, though it seemed strained. His eyes were dull, as though he hadn't slept in days. "What's going on? You don't look like you've been getting much rest."

Jonas forced a smile, trying to mask the unease that churned in his stomach. "I've been better, Daniel. But, uh, I need your help. We need to talk about the Thorpe case."

Daniel's face went blank. "Thorpe case?" he repeated, the words hanging in the air. He furrowed his brow as if trying to recall something distant, but there was nothing there. No recognition. No flicker of familiarity. "I'm sorry, but I don't know what you're talking about. I haven't worked on a Thorpe case."

The words hit Jonas like a punch in the gut. He couldn't hide the shock that must have been visible on his face. "What do you mean you haven't worked on it? We worked on it together, Daniel! We were preparing the defense, the evidence we'd uncovered—it was all right there. Don't you remember?"

Daniel shook his head slowly, his expression turning apologetic, though it felt hollow. "I don't remember any of that, Jonas. I haven't worked with you on any case like that. Maybe you're confused?"

Jonas blinked, disoriented. "Confused? No, no I'm not. We've been colleagues for years. You know this case, you know Damien Thorpe is innocent—God, Daniel, we've been over all of this together." His voice was rising now, panic creeping in. He reached for a stack of papers on Daniel's desk, the papers related to the Thorpe case, hoping that seeing them would trigger something. Anything. "Look at this! You signed this affidavit!"

Daniel stared at the papers as if they were completely foreign to him. His eyes flicked over the text briefly, and then his gaze returned to Jonas. "I don't know what you're talking about. I've never signed that. And honestly, I don't even know who Damien Thorpe is."

Jonas stepped back, his heart pounding in his chest. His mind raced, trying to process what was happening. "This is insane," he muttered. "We've worked together for years. How can you not remember?"

Daniel leaned back in his chair, his face unreadable. "Look,

I'm not sure what you're going through, but I think you need to take a step back. Maybe you've been under too much pressure. You need a break. A fresh perspective."

Jonas stared at him, feeling the walls of reality begin to crack. This wasn't possible. This couldn't be happening. He had known Daniel for years—knew his mannerisms, his quirks. They had shared countless cases, fought together in courtrooms. And yet, here he was, standing in front of a man who didn't even recognize him or the case they had worked on. The confusion, the unease, it was all too much.

"Are you sure about this?" Jonas asked, his voice barely above a whisper. "Is this some kind of joke? Are you part of it? Are you part of what's happening? This is all connected, Daniel. The disappearances, the altered records, the evidence vanishing—I think we're dealing with something far bigger than you or I could have imagined."

Daniel's eyes flickered for a brief moment, but the expression faded before Jonas could read it. "I don't know what you're talking about. But maybe you should go home, get some rest. Get your mind right."

Jonas felt a chill creep up his spine. He had never seen Daniel like this. There was no empathy in his voice, no warmth in his words. It was as if the man sitting in front of him wasn't the person he had known for years, but a complete stranger.

Jonas turned and walked out of the office, his mind reeling. He had no idea what was happening, but he could feel the sharp edges of panic starting to grip him. Everything he had worked for, everything he believed in, was slipping away. The people he trusted were disappearing, his own memories were faltering, and the case he was fighting for was vanishing before his eyes.

As he made his way down the hallway, he passed by other

colleagues, but none of them seemed to notice him. No one looked up, no one acknowledged his presence. It was as if he was invisible. He stopped in his tracks and glanced back over his shoulder, half-expecting to see someone behind him, someone who knew what was happening. But no one came.

Jonas pulled out his phone, fingers shaking, and dialed Samira's number. It rang twice before her voice came through on the line.

"Jonas? What's wrong?"

"Samira…" Jonas said, his voice cracking. "Something's wrong. I just spoke to Daniel—he doesn't remember anything. He doesn't remember the Thorpe case. He doesn't even remember me. This is happening again, and I don't know what's real anymore."

A silence fell over the line. For a moment, Jonas thought Samira might say something, but then she spoke, her voice calm but filled with concern. "Jonas, listen to me. This is bigger than we thought. You need to be careful. I've been looking into it, and I think I've uncovered something. It's not just the cases that are disappearing, Jonas. It's people. Your memories, your colleagues—it's all being erased."

"Erased?" Jonas whispered, his heart pounding in his chest. "What does that even mean?"

"I don't know, but I'm working on it. You need to get out of there. Get away from the office. We need to regroup, figure this out together. I'll keep digging. But be careful, Jonas. Whoever is behind this—they're watching."

As the call ended, Jonas stood there, staring at his phone. He felt an overwhelming sense of dread settle over him. He had been part of this system for so long, a defender of justice. But now, that system was crumbling. The very fabric of reality was slipping away, and Jonas wasn't sure if he could stop it.

The world was changing, erasing the truth one piece at a time. And Jonas wasn't sure if he was the last man standing—or if he was the next to disappear.

Ten

The Truth Unravels

Jonas Hale leaned back in his chair, staring at the papers scattered across his desk. The weight of the case pressed down on him, heavier than any trial he had faced before. Each document was a piece of a puzzle that didn't quite fit, each piece more disturbing than the last. He had thought he was fighting for justice. But now, the very system he had devoted his career to seemed to be crumbling, and he was starting to realize that he wasn't just fighting a case. He was fighting for his own existence.

The door to his office creaked open, and Jonas looked up. Samira Cross and Ethan Voss stood in the doorway, their faces grim, their eyes carrying the weight of everything they had uncovered.

"I found something," Samira said, her voice steady but with an edge of urgency. "Something that might explain all of this."

Jonas nodded, feeling a flicker of hope for the first time in days. The investigation had gone from strange to terrifying, but Samira's arrival had brought with it the possibility that they might be able to unravel the truth. Ethan stepped inside, closing the door behind him. He didn't speak at first, but Jonas could see the tension in his shoulders, the unease in his eyes.

"What did you find?" Jonas asked, his voice low, betraying his impatience.

Samira placed a folder on the desk in front of him. "This," she said. "I've been digging into the connections between Voryx Technologies and the cases that have been disappearing, and I stumbled across something chilling."

Jonas's heart skipped a beat at the mention of Voryx Technologies. The tech company's involvement had been a nagging thought in the back of his mind ever since he'd started investigating Damien Thorpe's case. The fact that Vera Novak, the murder victim, had ties to Voryx was no coincidence. But this... this was something different.

He opened the folder and scanned the papers inside. They were technical, full of jargon and convoluted legalese, but there was one thing that stood out: a series of transactions linked to Voryx Technologies, but the recipients of these transactions weren't companies or individuals—just anonymous codes.

"This doesn't make any sense," Jonas muttered, his brow furrowed as he continued reading. "Why would they hide this? And who are these codes supposed to represent?"

"That's the part that scares me," Samira said. "I traced the codes back to a small, private server. It's a digital footprint, but it's not just money being moved around. It's data. They're erasing history, Jonas."

Jonas's pulse quickened as the implications of Samira's words sank in. "Erasing history? You mean, like altering records?

Changing events?"

"Exactly," Samira replied. "But it's not just records, Jonas. It's everything. People's lives, memories. It's not just legal documents or evidence that's disappearing—it's entire histories. If these transactions are anything to go by, Voryx Technologies is at the heart of it all."

Jonas ran a hand through his hair, trying to wrap his mind around it. "How does it work? How can they alter history?"

Ethan spoke up, his voice low and deliberate. "I did some digging of my own. Voryx isn't just a tech company. They're using AI technology—advanced algorithms that can alter data, rewrite facts, and even manipulate people's memories. It's not just about controlling the past. It's about controlling the future, too."

Samira nodded. "The Revisionists—the shadowy group that's been pulling the strings—are using this technology to control the course of history. They don't just erase evidence or manipulate the present—they're erasing the very people who might expose the truth. They're making people disappear, Jonas. But it's more than just physical disappearance. They're making people forget."

Jonas felt a chill run through him. The idea of memory manipulation was something out of science fiction, but as Samira and Ethan spoke, he couldn't shake the feeling that everything was falling into place in the most terrifying way.

"So, the people who have been disappearing—who've had their memories erased—they're part of the plan?" Jonas asked, his voice strained.

"Yes," Ethan replied. "It's not just about erasing records. It's about rewriting people's lives. It's as if they've gone back and changed things, rewrote who people are. And it's not just the people involved in the cases. It's anyone who might stand in the way."

Jonas looked down at the papers in front of him, the weight of the truth pressing down on him. The pieces were coming together now, but it was a picture he wasn't sure he wanted to see.

"I don't understand," he said, his voice thick with disbelief. "How could they get away with this? How could something this big happen without anyone noticing?"

"They've been doing it for years," Samira said, her tone cold and resolute. "The Revisionists have been working in the shadows, slowly manipulating events. They control the systems, the people, the information. The more they erase, the more they can manipulate the future."

Jonas felt a knot tighten in his stomach. He had known the system was corrupt, but this… this was something far more sinister.

"What does this mean for the case?" he asked, his voice barely above a whisper.

Samira's eyes met his, and for the first time, Jonas saw a flicker of fear in her gaze. "It means your life—your career—everything you've worked for is at risk. They're erasing people who know too much, Jonas. And they're not going to stop."

Ethan stepped forward, his expression hardening. "The problem is, Jonas, you're not just fighting for Damien Thorpe anymore. You're fighting for yourself. You've been pulled into this web of lies, whether you realize it or not. And the Revisionists? They've been erasing your history, too."

Jonas's heart skipped a beat as the weight of Ethan's words sank in. His life, his past, everything he had worked for—was it all just a fabrication? Was he being erased, too?

"You don't mean that, right?" Jonas asked, his voice trembling with disbelief. "I've been a lawyer for years. I've defended criminals, yes, but I've always tried to do what's right. I've built my life on this. You can't just—"

"We're not saying your life is a lie, Jonas," Samira interjected, her voice soft but firm. "But the Revisionists have a way of altering what people believe is true. They make you forget. They make you question everything you've ever known."

Jonas looked down at the papers in front of him again, the words blurring on the page. The case had gone from strange to terrifying in the blink of an eye, and now it felt like his whole world was unraveling.

"Then what do we do?" he asked, the weight of responsibility pressing down on him. "How do we stop this? How do we fight something that can rewrite history itself?"

Samira's gaze hardened, and for the first time, Jonas saw the determination in her eyes. "We fight it by exposing the truth, Jonas. The truth that they're trying to hide. We find out who they really are, and we take them down."

Ethan nodded, his jaw clenched. "It won't be easy. But we have to move fast. The longer we wait, the more they'll erase."

Jonas took a deep breath and looked up at his two allies. He didn't know if they could win, or if they were walking into a trap. But one thing was certain: he couldn't back down now. The truth was out there, and if he had to burn everything to uncover it, he would.

"Let's do it," Jonas said, his voice steady, though his insides churned with doubt. "Let's find the Revisionists. And let's make sure they don't erase anyone else."

Eleven

The Illusion of Justice

Jonas Hale had always believed in the law. It had been the foundation of his career, the unwavering principle that guided his every move. As a defense attorney, he'd always prided himself on upholding the rights of the accused, ensuring that even the most despicable criminals had their day in court. The system was flawed, sure, but it was the best they had. Or so he'd always told himself.

But as the investigation into Damien Thorpe's case deepened, Jonas found himself standing on the edge of something far darker. He had started this journey thinking he was defending an innocent man, someone wronged by the justice system. But now, with each passing day, the truth had become murkier, and the line between right and wrong had started to blur. The more he uncovered about The Revisionists, the more he realized that he wasn't just fighting for Damien's freedom—he was fighting to hold onto his own sense of identity.

The walls of his office seemed to close in as Jonas sat at his desk, the weight of everything pressing down on him. The case that had started as a simple defense of a man accused of murder had spiraled into a labyrinth of corruption, manipulation, and hidden forces beyond his control. And the deeper he dug, the more he realized that he wasn't just an innocent bystander. He had been a part of it all along.

Damien Thorpe wasn't just the victim of a broken system—he was a victim of something far worse, something far more insidious. The more Jonas uncovered, the more it became clear: The Revisionists, the shadowy group manipulating the justice system, had been controlling his life in ways he couldn't even comprehend.

He stood up from his desk, pacing the room as his mind raced. The illusion of justice was starting to unravel before him, piece by piece, and there was no way to put it back together. He had been a pawn in a game he hadn't even realized he was playing.

Jonas's thoughts were interrupted by a knock at the door. He didn't need to look up to know who it was. Samira Cross had been a constant presence in his life since the investigation had started. She had been relentless in her pursuit of the truth, and in many ways, her unwavering determination had kept him grounded. But even she seemed to be changing. She, too, was starting to see the cracks in the system, and as much as she hated to admit it, Jonas could see the toll it was taking on her.

"Come in," Jonas called, his voice hoarse.

Samira entered the room, her face pale, her eyes shadowed with exhaustion. She had been up all night, going through the evidence, piecing together the fragmented pieces of the puzzle they were both trapped in. But even as she stepped inside, Jonas could see that something was different. She wasn't the same woman who had walked into his office weeks ago, determined to expose the truth. The weight of everything they had uncovered was starting to show.

"What is it?" Jonas asked, his voice tired but steady.

Samira hesitated for a moment, looking as though she was choosing her words carefully. When she finally spoke, her voice was quiet but firm.

"It's worse than we thought," she said. "The Revisionists are more embedded in the system than we realized. They control more than just the trials—they control the entire judicial process. Every part of it. And I think we've been played."

Jonas's stomach twisted. "Played?" he repeated. "What do you mean?"

Samira stepped forward, placing a folder on his desk. "I've been looking into the judges, the juries, the prosecutors. They're all connected—every single one of them. And it's not just about the cases they've manipulated. It's about the people they've erased. They're rewriting entire histories, Jonas. And we've been part of it."

Jonas swallowed hard, his mind racing. "What do you mean 'we've been part of it'?"

"The cases we've been defending," Samira continued. "We've been fighting for the wrong side. These aren't innocent people we're trying to free. They're pawns in a much larger game. And we've been feeding into it. We've been part of the system that's been designed to protect the corrupt."

The words hit Jonas like a punch to the gut. He staggered back, his hand gripping the edge of his desk for support. His thoughts were a whirlwind, his mind struggling to process what Samira was saying.

"No," Jonas whispered, shaking his head. "That can't be true.

I've spent my whole life defending the system. I've fought for the truth, for justice."

"Jonas," Samira said softly, her voice full of empathy. "The system is broken. The truth you've been fighting for? It's been manipulated, altered, rewritten. And you've been defending it without even realizing it."

Jonas's hands trembled as he ran them through his hair, the weight of the truth settling in. He had always prided himself on being a defender of justice, but now he saw the ugly reality: He had been a tool, a cog in the very machine he had fought against for so long.

He looked up at Samira, his eyes filled with a mixture of fear and disbelief. "So what now? What do we do?"

Samira's expression was hard, her eyes burning with a resolve Jonas hadn't seen before. "We expose them. We take down The Revisionists, tear the system apart, and rebuild it from the ground up. It won't be easy, but it's the only way. We can't let them win, Jonas. Not now. Not when we're so close."

Jonas looked down at the folder Samira had placed on his desk. Inside was more evidence, more proof that the system he had spent his life fighting for was not what it seemed. It was a machine, a carefully crafted illusion, designed to manipulate the truth and erase those who got in the way.

He took a deep breath and straightened up, his mind made up. "You're right. We can't let them win. We'll expose them, no matter the cost."

Samira nodded. "We'll do it together. We're not alone in this."

Jonas looked at her, feeling a sense of determination wash over him. For the first time in days, he felt like he had a purpose again. The system was broken, but they could fix it. They could take down The Revisionists and expose the truth.

"We have to be careful," Jonas said, his voice steady but tinged with urgency. "If they're as powerful as we think, we won't be the only ones at risk. They'll come for us."

"I know," Samira said, her eyes narrowing. "But we can't back down. The truth is too important."

Jonas took one last look at the folder in front of him, then stood up and walked to the window. The city outside seemed quiet, peaceful even. But Jonas knew better now. Everything he thought he knew had been a lie, a carefully constructed illusion.

He turned to Samira, his jaw set with resolve. "Let's bring this down."

Samira smiled, the first glimmer of hope in her eyes. "Together, we will."

Twelve

The Rewritten Past

Jonas Hale sat alone in his office, the dim light of the desk lamp casting long shadows across the room. The case he had been so determined to unravel was slipping through his fingers, and the harder he tried to grasp it, the more the truth seemed to shift, just out of reach. Damien Thorpe's trial, the mysterious disappearances, the strange events that had been plaguing him—none of it made sense anymore.

But there was one name that kept resurfacing, one entity that seemed to be at the heart of it all: Voryx Technologies.

Jonas had tried to ignore it at first, dismissing it as just another corporate player in the background, something unrelated to the tangled web he was attempting to untangle. But every lead he followed, every new piece of information he uncovered, kept pointing him back to the same place. Voryx.

The company's influence was vast, its reach global, and its technology cutting-edge. But it wasn't the technology itself that worried Jonas. It was what the company was doing with it. His research into Voryx revealed something far more sinister—something that made his blood run cold.

Artificial intelligence, it seemed, was not just being used for convenience or efficiency. Voryx was using AI to manipulate history itself. They had developed algorithms capable of rewriting records, erasing people, altering memories, and even creating fabricated histories. In essence, Voryx had the power to control the very narrative of reality.

Jonas leaned back in his chair, his mind reeling with the implications of what he had just uncovered. If The Revisionists were using Voryx's technology to manipulate history, it meant that the trial of Damien Thorpe, the witness disappearances, the strange photos—they were all part of something much larger. Someone was controlling the very essence of truth itself, and Jonas had been caught in the middle of it. Worse, he was beginning to suspect that his own life—his past, his career— might not be his own anymore.

He ran his hands over his face, feeling the weight of the discovery settling on his shoulders. The truth was becoming impossible to ignore. The Revisionists weren't just manipulating the legal system—they were rewriting history, erasing people, and altering memories. Jonas's life was no exception.

As he sat in the silence of his office, the phone on his desk rang, breaking his train of thought. He stared at it for a moment before picking it up.

"Jonas Hale," he answered, his voice hoarse from the tension of the last few days.

"Jonas," came Samira's voice, sharp and urgent. "You're not going to believe what I found."

Jonas's heart skipped a beat. He'd been expecting her call, but the tone in her voice made him uneasy. "What is it?"

"I've been digging into Voryx Technologies. You're right about them," she said, her words quick and clipped. "But there's more to it. A lot more. It's not just a tech company—it's a front for a much larger operation."

Jonas felt a chill spread through him. "How much larger?"

"Let's just say that the entire company is involved in this. Voryx isn't just manipulating records—they're creating new realities. They have the technology to erase entire histories, fabricate people's identities, and change entire events. It's not just AI—it's the foundation for everything The Revisionists are doing."

Jonas's mind raced. He could feel the ground beneath him shifting. If Samira's information was correct, it meant that everything he had believed about his life, his career, even the case he was fighting for, could be nothing more than a construct of someone else's making. The Revisionists had the power to control it all, and now Jonas was beginning to realize just how deep their influence went.

"Are you saying they've been rewriting my life?" Jonas asked, his voice barely above a whisper.

"I'm afraid so," Samira replied. "And not just yours. They've been erasing people's histories, erasing entire families, changing the course of events. Your case with Damien Thorpe, the murder victim Vera Novak—those aren't isolated incidents. This is a systematic operation. They're erasing anyone who gets too close to the truth, manipulating the legal system, the media, and even history itself."

Jonas stood up, pacing the room. His mind spun with the enormity of it all. His instincts had been right—the case he was fighting wasn't just about defending a man accused of murder.

It was about something much bigger, something that threatened the very foundation of reality.

"Where does this leave us?" Jonas asked, his voice laced with desperation.

"We keep digging," Samira said, her voice resolute. "We expose them. We can't back down now, Jonas. The more we uncover, the closer we get to the truth. But we have to move fast. The longer we stay in the dark, the more likely they are to erase us, too."

Jonas nodded, determination flaring in his chest. They were up against something far more powerful than he had ever imagined, but he wasn't going to back down now. The stakes had never been higher. The Revisionists had already taken so much—his career, his identity, and even his understanding of reality itself. But Jonas wasn't going to let them win. He was going to expose them for what they were.

"I'll keep digging," Jonas said, his voice firm. "And I won't stop until we've destroyed this entire system."

"Good," Samira replied. "But be careful. Voryx Technologies isn't the only player in this game. There are others involved, and they're watching us."

Jonas gripped the edge of his desk, his knuckles white. He could feel the weight of the situation pressing down on him, but he knew one thing for sure: He wasn't alone in this fight. Samira, Ethan, and the few allies they had left were in this together. And no matter what, they were going to bring The Revisionists down.

As the conversation ended, Jonas's thoughts returned to the chilling truth he had uncovered. Voryx Technologies had the power to rewrite history itself. They could alter memories, erase people, and control the very narrative of reality. And

Jonas—Jonas was a part of that narrative. His past, his career, his very existence had been manipulated by forces beyond his control.

He turned back to his desk, his eyes falling on the case file for Damien Thorpe. The evidence was damning, but now Jonas knew that the real battle was not just to clear Damien's name— it was to fight back against the system that had created this nightmare in the first place.

The road ahead was uncertain, and Jonas knew that every step he took would bring him closer to danger. But he also knew that the truth had to come out. The Revisionists couldn't be allowed to rewrite history, to control the narrative, to erase the past. He would stand up to them, no matter the cost.

With a deep breath, Jonas sat back down at his desk, his fingers brushing over the pile of papers that had been the center of his investigation. There was no turning back now. The fight for justice had just begun, and Jonas was ready to take on whatever came next.

An Unexpected Ally

The fluorescent lights buzzed above Jonas Hale's desk, casting a sterile glow across the files that littered the surface. The weight of the case was suffocating, every document a reminder of the walls closing in around him. Damien Thorpe's case had spiraled into something much darker than a simple defense—Jonas had become entangled in a conspiracy that threatened to rewrite his entire existence.

He had started out as a lawyer, a defender of the innocent, but now, as he sifted through his notes, he wasn't sure what was real anymore. The faces of people he had once known—friends, colleagues, even family—seemed to blur, and memories of cases he had won, clients he had defended, felt like ghosts. He knew that The Revisionists were behind it all, pulling the strings from behind a curtain of lies and erased histories. And Jonas, for all his skill in the courtroom, was no match for them.

The phone on his desk rang, breaking through the silence

of his isolation. Jonas stared at it for a long moment, his fingers hovering above the receiver. He had no one left to turn to. Samira was buried in her own investigation, Ethan was following leads that led him further away, and the rest of his life had begun to fade, as if someone was intentionally erasing it.

He picked up the receiver.

"Jonas Hale," he answered, his voice hoarse.

"Jonas, it's me," came the voice on the other end, familiar yet unexpected.

Jonas sat up straighter, his pulse quickening. "What's this about?" he asked, trying to steady his voice.

"I'm not calling as an enemy, Jonas. I'm calling as a friend," the voice replied, the words laced with a certain urgency. "I've been watching everything unfold. You don't know me, but I know you. I've been inside the system. And I've seen it all."

Jonas furrowed his brow, the suspicion creeping in. He had no reason to trust this voice, no reason to believe anyone could be an ally in his fight. But there was something in the tone that kept him listening. "Who is this?" Jonas demanded, though his heart raced in anticipation.

"The name's Olivia Marks," the voice said, and Jonas's breath caught in his throat. Olivia Marks. The former prosecutor who had worked on several high-profile cases with him. They had crossed paths years ago, when he had worked as a defense attorney for a criminal syndicate she had been trying to bring down. He had despised her methods—cold, calculated, willing to bend the rules of justice to get the result she wanted.

But she had disappeared after a botched case, her career ruined after being implicated in a scandal involving The Revisionists. No one had heard from her since. Until now.

"You," Jonas whispered, disbelief creeping into his voice. "You've been on the inside all this time?"

"I had no choice," Olivia replied, her voice tight with regret. "I had to. The system… it was always broken. The Revisionists, they've been manipulating everything for years, even before you started uncovering the truth. But I've seen it now, Jonas. I've seen how deep the rot goes. I was one of them. I worked for them."

Jonas's mind raced. He remembered the stories—the whispers about a shadowy organization that controlled the legal world, bending the law to their will, erasing the truth. But he had always thought those stories were just that—stories, rumors. He never thought it was real, at least not until now. But the pieces were starting to fit. He had seen the changes in his own life, in his own memories. He had felt the system bend, contort around him. And now, Olivia was offering him a chance to fight back.

"You're telling me you want to help?" Jonas asked, incredulous. "You were one of them. How can I trust you?"

"I know I'm asking a lot," Olivia said, her voice heavy with guilt. "But I've had enough. I've seen the destruction they've caused. I've been part of it. But now, I'm ready to help you take them down. I know where their secrets are hidden, and I have access to things that could expose them—things they thought no one could touch."

Jonas's thoughts were a whirl of confusion and disbelief. Olivia Marks had always been a formidable opponent. She was ruthless, a woman driven by ambition and power. But now she was offering him a lifeline. Could he trust her?

"Why now?" Jonas asked, his voice low. "Why are you coming to me now, after everything?"

"I've been watching," Olivia replied. "I saw the pieces coming together, and I realized something. You're the only one who can stop them. They've already started erasing you, Jonas. Your life, your career—it's all been manipulated. But there's still time. There's a way to fight back. But you need to act fast."

Jonas's heart pounded in his chest. He had suspected that someone was pulling the strings, but hearing it confirmed by Olivia was both a shock and a wake-up call. She had been inside the system, and now, she was offering him a chance to fight back.

"What do you want from me?" Jonas asked, his voice steady, but with an edge of suspicion. "What's your endgame?"

"My endgame?" Olivia scoffed, a bitter laugh escaping her lips. "I'm not asking for anything from you, Jonas. I'm asking for you to help me expose them. You've got the pieces—now, I can help you put them together. But you have to trust me."

Jonas closed his eyes, rubbing his temples as the weight of the decision began to settle on him. Everything had been leading to this moment, but the stakes had never been higher. The Revisionists were powerful, and they were everywhere. Jonas had seen how they had destroyed everything he had worked for. But now, Olivia Marks—the woman who had once been his adversary—was offering him a chance to turn the tide.

"How do I know you're not setting me up?" Jonas asked, his voice laced with doubt. "How do I know this isn't just another trap?"

"I understand why you're cautious," Olivia said softly. "I wouldn't expect anything less. But listen to me, Jonas. If we don't act now, they will erase us. The truth will disappear, and we'll be nothing more than forgotten pawns in their game."

Jonas felt the weight of her words. He had spent years

defending the law, but now he was realizing that the law itself was broken, twisted beyond recognition. It was no longer about justice—it was about control. And he had been living in the lie for far too long.

"I'll meet you," Jonas said, his voice firm with resolve. "But I need to know everything. If I'm going to take this fight to them, I need to know exactly what I'm up against."

"I'll explain everything when we meet," Olivia replied. "There's a safe house. I'll send you the details. Get there as soon as you can."

The line went dead, and Jonas sat back in his chair, his mind spinning. He had always been a man of reason, of logic. But now, his world had been shattered, and he was faced with a choice that could change everything. Could he trust Olivia? Or was this all part of a larger game, one that had been playing him all along?

The answer was clear: He didn't have a choice. The Revisionists were controlling the narrative, erasing people's histories, and rewriting the law. If Jonas didn't act now, everything he had worked for—his career, his life—would be erased, too.

Jonas stood up, his hands trembling. He had a decision to make, and there was no turning back. The game had changed, and he was about to be part of something much bigger than he had ever imagined.

He grabbed his coat and headed for the door, determined to meet Olivia Marks and find the truth, no matter where it led.

Fourteen

The Hidden Hand

The streets of Eridale were colder than usual, the wind biting through Jonas Hale's coat as he navigated the labyrinth of alleys and narrow streets. The city, with its gothic architecture and beautiful, yet haunting, façades, felt more like a graveyard than a thriving metropolis. He had spent years working within this system, believing in the law, in justice. But now, as he ventured deeper into this conspiracy, the truth was becoming unbearable.

His meeting was set for 9:00 PM, in an abandoned office building on the outskirts of the city. A place where shadows clung to the walls, where every floorboard creaked underfoot, and where the air was thick with the weight of untold secrets. Jonas's heart beat a little faster as he approached the building, knowing that the person waiting for him inside could finally provide the answers he'd been desperately seeking.

For weeks, he'd been chasing down fragments of information,

piecing together the tangled web of The Revisionists—a secret organization with the power to alter history, erase memories, and manipulate entire legal systems. And now, a man named Victor Westbrook, a former member of The Revisionists, had agreed to meet him. He was the first to admit the organization's existence. The first to acknowledge the power they wielded. He was the key to understanding the full extent of the manipulation and how deep the corruption went. But Jonas wasn't naïve. He knew Westbrook wasn't offering this information out of the goodness of his heart.

"Be careful, Jonas," Samira had warned earlier that day. "You're treading dangerous ground. The deeper you go, the harder it will be to get out."

Jonas understood the gravity of her words. But there was no turning back now. The pieces were all there, and this was his only chance to understand who was behind the erasure of people's lives—his life included. Who controlled The Revisionists? Who pulled the strings? And why had Damien Thorpe been chosen as the sacrificial pawn in their twisted game?

As he stepped into the darkened lobby of the building, the faint smell of mildew filled his nostrils. The building had been abandoned for years, but this was the meeting place Victor Westbrook had chosen. No one would be able to track them here. Jonas checked his watch—8:55 PM. He had five minutes before the meeting.

Taking a deep breath, he proceeded down the hall toward the elevators, his footsteps echoing in the empty space. As he approached the door marked "Office 302," he heard the sound of footsteps behind him. He turned, but there was no one there.

His heart skipped a beat.

"Paranoia," he muttered under his breath. He hadn't been followed, he told himself. This was just the nerves getting to him.

The door to the office creaked open as Jonas approached. He stepped inside cautiously, scanning the room for any sign of danger. Westbrook was sitting at a table in the center of the room, a glass of whiskey in front of him. The man looked as if he hadn't slept in days—his hair was unkempt, his suit rumpled. But his eyes were sharp, alert.

"You came," Westbrook said, his voice hoarse but steady. He didn't stand to greet Jonas.

"I wasn't sure you'd show," Jonas replied, locking the door behind him. "How do I know this isn't a trap?"

Westbrook smiled bitterly. "You're already in too deep for it to be a trap, Hale. You wouldn't have come this far if you weren't already a part of their game. But I'm not here to play games. I'm here to tell you what I know."

Jonas pulled out a chair and sat down across from Westbrook. "Let's get to it then. What do you know about The Revisionists? About their reach, their motives?"

Westbrook sighed and took a long gulp of whiskey before setting the glass down. "The Revisionists are not just some underground organization—they're the ones pulling the strings in every part of society. They control politics, they control business, they control the media, and most of all—they control the law. They've been erasing history for decades, manipulating events, and altering outcomes to fit their vision of the future. And they're not afraid to kill to protect their secrets."

Jonas leaned forward, his mind racing. "Why? What's their endgame?"

"Their goal is control," Westbrook said, his voice low. "They believe in a new world order, one where history is malleable. The truth is whatever they say it is. And they've been using technology to make it happen. Voryx Technologies is their weapon of choice. The AI they've developed allows them to alter records, delete memories, even manipulate people's perceptions. Everything you've ever known—the cases you've worked on, the people you've defended—all of it could have been changed without you ever knowing."

Jonas felt a chill run down his spine. "Voryx Technologies? The tech company? That's how they're doing it?"

Westbrook nodded. "They've infiltrated every level of society, Jonas. Voryx's technology allows them to rewrite history in ways we can't even begin to understand. People's lives are erased, people's pasts are manipulated, and no one is any the wiser. It's like living in a world where reality is constantly shifting."

Jonas's mind whirled with the implications. He had seen the evidence of it already. Damien's case. The missing witnesses. The erased files. It was all connected to The Revisionists, and it all led back to Voryx.

"So, what now?" Jonas asked, his voice tight with urgency. "How do we stop them?"

Westbrook stared at him for a long moment. "That's the question, isn't it? I've been trying to figure it out for years. But there's a problem. The Revisionists don't just erase people— they erase everything about them. You think they've left a trail? Think again. They've made sure no one remembers them, no one knows who they really are. They've created a world where their fingerprints are invisible. And now… now, they're coming for you."

Jonas's pulse quickened. "What do you mean?"

"Don't trust anyone, Hale," Westbrook warned, his voice shaking. "They're watching you. They've been watching you for weeks. Every move you make is being tracked. Every conversation you have is being listened to. They've already started to rewrite your life, just like they've done with everyone else. You're already a part of their game."

Jonas stood abruptly, the weight of Westbrook's words sinking in. "This isn't over. You can't just tell me this and walk away. If they're watching me, they're going to come for you, too."

Westbrook shook his head. "It's too late for me. But it's not too late for you, Jonas. You have to stop them, before they erase everything. Before they erase you."

Suddenly, there was a knock at the door.

Jonas's heart skipped a beat. "Who is it?" he called out, his voice laced with suspicion.

But there was no answer. The door creaked open, and Jonas froze.

A figure stood in the doorway, cloaked in shadow.

Before Jonas could react, the figure lunged, a gloved hand clamping over his mouth, silencing his scream. The last thing he heard was Westbrook's desperate shout, "Get out of here, now!"

And then, everything went black.

The next morning, Jonas awoke in a different place entirely—no longer in the abandoned office but in a nondescript hotel room. His body ached, his mind foggy. He stumbled to the window and looked outside, only to find a different cityscape staring back at him.

It wasn't Eridale.

His heart pounded in his chest, and his stomach dropped. Something was terribly wrong.

He didn't know how, but The Revisionists had already made their move. They'd erased another piece of his reality.

Jonas had been marked, and now, he was running out of time.

Fifteen

Facing the Consequences

The weight of the decision settled heavily on Jonas's shoulders. As he stood at the window of his cramped apartment in the heart of Eridale, looking out at the dimly lit city, his mind raced. The forces behind The Revisionists were closing in on him, on Samira, on Ethan—on all of them. They were no longer just faceless shadows manipulating the legal system; they were real, tangible threats, and they were coming for them.

Jonas knew he couldn't afford to wait any longer. He had seen enough to understand that their lives were at risk. The Revisionists weren't just rewriting history—they were erasing the very existence of those who dared to challenge them. He had already begun to see the cracks in his own life, the moments when reality itself started to splinter. His name was being erased from records, his identity dissolved into the void. And the worst part? He could feel it—feel the pull of the void, the creeping certainty that his time was running out.

His phone buzzed on the table, pulling him from his dark thoughts. It was a message from Samira.

We need to meet. They know we're onto them.

Jonas's heart skipped a beat. Samira's words were a stark reminder of the stakes. It wasn't just the case they were up against anymore. It wasn't just about Damien Thorpe or Voryx Technologies or the invisible hand of The Revisionists. It was about survival. About whether they could fight back or whether they were doomed to be forgotten.

He had to make a choice.

Jonas grabbed his coat, his fingers trembling as he buttoned it up. It was time to face the consequences. Whatever came next, he couldn't hide any longer. They couldn't hide any longer.

As Jonas made his way to the meeting point—an abandoned café on the outskirts of the city—his mind kept turning over the same question: *Do we expose them? Or do we disappear?*

The city, with its cobbled streets and winding alleyways, felt more sinister than it ever had before. Eridale had always had a dark edge to it—its beauty, like a mask, hiding the rotting core beneath—but now, every corner seemed to hold a threat. Every shadow, a reminder that they were being watched. That they were being hunted.

He arrived at the café, a dilapidated building that had seen better days. The windows were cracked, the door barely hanging on its hinges. Inside, the flickering lights cast long shadows over the empty tables. Samira was already there, sitting in the farthest corner, her back to the wall, eyes scanning the room. Ethan was beside her, his usual air of confident determination replaced by something darker—something weary.

Jonas slid into the seat across from them. He didn't say

anything at first, just took a long look at the two people who had been with him through this nightmare.

"We're being hunted," Samira said quietly, her voice heavy with urgency. "Every move we make is being tracked."

Jonas nodded, trying to steady his nerves. "We're already dead to them. If we don't make a decision, we'll be erased. All of us."

Ethan leaned forward, his brow furrowed. "Exposing them would mean risking everything—our lives, our futures. But hiding? That's just a temporary solution. They'll come for us eventually, no matter where we go."

"Do we even have a choice?" Jonas muttered. His mind was spinning, overwhelmed by the enormity of the situation. "We've seen too much. The truth is out there, but so are we. Exposing them might give us a shot at stopping this—at preventing more people from getting erased. But they'll never let us expose them."

"The question is," Samira said, her gaze unwavering, "what do we stand to lose? If we run, if we disappear, we might save our lives for a while. But the system we're fighting for—justice, the truth—it's already dead. The Revisionists have taken it. But if we expose them, we risk everything. We risk being wiped from existence. What happens to the truth when no one can remember it?"

A heavy silence fell over the table. It was a question none of them wanted to answer, but they all knew it was the truth: exposing The Revisionists could cost them everything. It could cost them their names, their memories, their very existence.

Jonas rubbed his temples, trying to focus. The pieces were all there—the erased cases, the missing witnesses, the altered memories. Voryx Technologies, the AI, the rewriting of history—it was all tied together. But how could they prove it? How could they expose something that was so insidious, so thoroughly embedded in every part of the world?

"The truth is," Jonas said, breaking the silence, "we're fighting an enemy we can't even see. The Revisionists control everything—the legal system, the media, the very narrative we're living in. We're just pawns in their game. But if we don't expose them now, if we don't take a stand, we'll lose. Not just our lives, but the entire system of justice."

Ethan stood, pacing around the room. "So what are we doing? Are we fighting to the end? Or are we going underground, trying to survive this thing and hope for the best?"

Samira's eyes met Jonas's, and for the first time in what felt like forever, Jonas saw something in her gaze—something close to resolve. She wasn't afraid of dying. She wasn't afraid of being erased. She was afraid of the world that would continue if they did nothing. If they let The Revisionists win.

"We expose them," Samira said, her voice steady but full of determination. "We risk it all. The truth is too important to bury. We can't let them control the narrative any longer."

Jonas took a deep breath. It was the only choice they had. There was no turning back now.

"We go public," Jonas said, his voice resolute. "We expose Voryx Technologies, The Revisionists—everything. We take this fight to the world."

Ethan stopped pacing and looked at both of them. "This could get us killed, you know. It could erase everything we've worked for. Everything we are. We won't just lose our lives. We'll be erased from history."

"I know," Jonas said quietly. "But if we don't do this, if we don't expose them, we'll lose something far worse. We'll lose the truth."

The weight of their decision settled over them, heavy and suffocating. They were on the precipice now, standing at the edge of a cliff with no way back. Jonas knew that this was it. They had chosen their path, and the consequences would be grave.

"You're sure about this?" Samira asked, her voice a whisper now. "This is our only shot."

Jonas nodded. "There's no going back. If we want to fix this, if we want to save the truth, we have to expose them now."

For a long moment, no one spoke. The world outside the café seemed distant, as if they were no longer a part of it. The decision had been made. Their fates were sealed.

Ethan turned, pulling out his phone. "I'll get the media involved. If we're going down, we're taking them with us."

Jonas stood up, his legs unsteady. He had no idea what they were about to face, but one thing was clear—they were going to need all the help they could get.

And so, as the storm of The Revisionists began to close in, Jonas Hale, Samira Cross, and Ethan Voss prepared to take their fight to the very heart of the conspiracy, risking everything to expose the truth. But as they walked into the unknown, they knew one thing for certain: their lives would never be the same again.

Sixteen

Rewriting the Rules

The clock ticked in the corner of Jonas's office, the rhythmic sound filling the space between his scattered thoughts. It was late—far too late for anyone to still be awake, and yet, here he was, unable to shake the horrifying realization that had gripped him earlier that day. His investigation into The Revisionists, the shadowy group responsible for manipulating the truth, had already led him down dark, winding paths, but what he was beginning to uncover now was more sinister than anything he could have imagined.

The files in front of him blurred as his mind raced. What if everything he had believed was a lie? What if his entire career, his entire life, had been part of their manipulation? He had always prided himself on being a lawyer who fought for the truth, no matter the odds. But now, as he pieced together the puzzle, he began to wonder if the rules had always been rigged against him.

The Revisionists aren't just rewriting history... they're rewriting everything.

That thought echoed in his mind like a curse.

Jonas leaned forward, scanning the scattered papers on his desk. He had spent hours combing through them, each file a piece of the puzzle, each detail another link in the chain that led back to Voryx Technologies. The AI company that had once seemed like a mere footnote in his investigation now loomed larger than ever, its connections to The Revisionists growing clearer by the minute.

His phone buzzed, interrupting his thoughts. It was Samira. *We need to talk. You're getting too close.*

The message made him pause. He had already crossed so many lines in the investigation. Every new lead, every revelation only seemed to take him deeper into the heart of a conspiracy that spanned not just criminal trials but entire histories, people's lives, and memories. But Samira's words struck a chord. He was getting too close to something, something that was no longer just a case to be solved but a dangerous web that entangled everything he knew.

He took a deep breath and dialed Samira's number. She picked up on the first ring.

"Jonas," she said, her voice low and urgent. "You're digging in the wrong place. You're starting to uncover things that should stay buried."

Jonas's grip tightened around the phone. "I know what they're doing, Samira. This isn't just about the law anymore. They're rewriting history—reprogramming people's memories, their identities. It's like they're playing God."

There was a pause on the other end. Jonas could practically

hear the wheels turning in her head. "I know. But you need to stop. You're beginning to unravel something bigger than you can handle. It's not just the trial, or Voryx Technologies. The Revisionists… they control more than you think."

His pulse quickened. "What do you mean, 'they control more than I think'?"

"They're not just erasing people from history, Jonas. They're rewriting *everything*—not just records, but memories, identities, people's entire lives. They've been doing it for years. And now, they're coming for you."

Jonas's thoughts raced. "Coming for me? What are you talking about?"

"I'm saying, Jonas, they've already started rewriting your past. The way you remember things—your career, your history, your own identity. Everything you think you know about yourself might not be true. Everything you've uncovered might be part of their plan."

A cold shiver ran down Jonas's spine. He stood up abruptly, pacing back and forth. "What do you mean? How could they have done that?"

"It's the power of the technology they control," Samira said, her voice tight. "AI. Memory manipulation. You've seen the way Voryx Technologies works. You think it's just a tech company? It's much more than that. They have the ability to alter memories—yours, mine, anyone's. They can change our lives, rewrite our history, and we wouldn't even know it."

Jonas froze, his thoughts grinding to a halt. *They can change our lives... rewrite our history...*

The realization hit him like a punch to the stomach. If they could rewrite his past, how could he trust anything he remembered? What if his entire life had been a carefully constructed illusion, created by these unseen forces?

His hands trembled as he sat back down, trying to steady his mind. "This doesn't make sense. Why me? Why now?"

Samira's voice softened. "Because you're asking the right questions. You're getting too close. You're starting to uncover the truth behind The Revisionists, and they don't like that. You're a threat to everything they've built. And the more you dig, the more they'll erase."

Jonas closed his eyes, the weight of the situation bearing down on him. "So what do I do? How do I fight something like this?"

"You have to expose them, Jonas. That's the only way. But you have to be careful. The closer you get, the more they'll try to erase you."

Jonas's mind reeled. He was already losing his grip on reality—on what was real and what was fabricated. The case, Damien Thorpe, Voryx Technologies—it was all connected, he could feel it in his gut. But how much of it was real? How much of his past, his very identity, had been altered by The Revisionists? And how much of this was part of their grand design?

The line went quiet for a moment, and then Samira spoke again. "Jonas, I've found something. A lead. You need to meet me. I have something that might help you understand just how deep this goes."

Jonas's heart raced. "Where?"

"Meet me at the old courthouse. The one on the outskirts of the city. Midnight. Don't bring anyone."

He hung up the phone, his mind buzzing with a thousand questions. Samira had always been a reliable ally, but now, with everything that had been happening, Jonas wasn't sure who he could trust. If Voryx Technologies was behind all of this, if The Revisionists controlled the very fabric of reality, how could anyone stand against them?

He had to meet Samira. He had to get to the bottom of this. The truth was slipping further away, but Jonas knew he couldn't stop. Not now. He had to expose them before they erased everything. Before they erased *him*.

As the clock ticked down to midnight, Jonas left his office, his mind clouded with doubt and fear. He had to confront The Revisionists. He had to find out who they were, what they wanted, and what their ultimate goal was. But with every step he took toward the courthouse, the reality of his situation became clearer: the more he dug, the more he uncovered, the closer he came to becoming just another erased memory in a world rewritten by those who controlled the truth.

And yet, he had no choice. He couldn't let them win. He couldn't let them erase him.

Jonas Hale had to fight. And he would fight with everything he had left.

Seventeen

The Endgame Approaches

The city was dark, the streets quiet, but Jonas felt the weight of every footstep he took. Samira had led them through a labyrinth of hidden pathways and forgotten corners of Eridale. The final leg of their journey felt suffocating, each alley and side street seeming more ominous than the last. They were close—so close to unmasking The Revisionists, to ending the game they had been playing for so long. Yet, with each passing moment, Jonas was beginning to wonder just how much he could trust his own senses.

As they approached the derelict building at the end of the road, Jonas looked at Samira and Ethan, both of them as tense as he was. The stakes had never been higher. If they were wrong about this meeting, if they failed to expose the truth, it wouldn't just be the case they were fighting for. It wouldn't just be their lives that were at risk. No, this time, the very fabric of reality itself would be at stake. And they might not even remember they had fought.

Inside the building, the air was stale, the lights flickering intermittently, casting long shadows on the walls. They entered a large room, an underground chamber filled with computers, books, and large tables scattered with papers. But it wasn't the technology that caught Jonas's attention—it was the figures seated around a table in the center of the room, staring at them.

For a moment, Jonas hesitated, the heavy silence almost suffocating him. There were six people in the room, and they were watching the trio with unsettling intensity. One of them, a man in his fifties, nodded towards Jonas, as if welcoming him.

"You're late," he said, his voice calm but with an edge of authority that made Jonas's skin crawl.

"Who are you?" Samira demanded, her hand subtly moving toward her side, where a weapon might lie hidden. Ethan's hand twitched as well, and Jonas knew that this was the moment of truth. The confrontation was inevitable, but now that it was here, Jonas felt his pulse quicken. This wasn't just about exposing The Revisionists anymore—it was about survival.

The man smiled, a cold, almost cruel smile. "I'm someone who's seen your little game for what it is, Samira. Jonas, Ethan, you've played your parts well. But you're too late."

Jonas narrowed his eyes, glancing at Samira and Ethan. He could feel the tension mounting. This was the moment they had all been working towards—the moment they would either expose the conspiracy or fall into it. And yet, there was something about this man's voice, his demeanor, that made Jonas uneasy. This wasn't a mere criminal syndicate—they weren't just operating on a legal plane anymore. There was something darker, something far more dangerous, beneath the surface.

"Too late?" Jonas repeated, trying to steady his breath. "What's going on here? Who are you people?"

The man leaned forward, resting his hands on the table. "We are The Revisionists, the architects of history itself. You've been chasing shadows, thinking you're exposing a conspiracy of criminals, but you're wrong. We're not just rewriting criminal cases. We're rewriting everything."

Jonas felt his blood run cold at the realization. They weren't just changing court cases. They were rewriting the entire world. History. Society. The very events that shaped their reality.

"The courts. The laws. The people you thought were innocent or guilty," the man continued, his voice almost hypnotic. "It's all an illusion. We make the decisions. We control the narrative. We decide what you remember and what you forget."

Samira's voice cut through the tension. "But why? Why do this? What's the purpose?"

The man didn't answer right away. Instead, he looked at the others around the table, nodding slowly, as if gathering their approval before continuing. "Because the truth is malleable, Samira. The truth is a tool, a weapon, and we've learned how to wield it. All of you—your lives, your histories, your very identities—are just parts of a larger experiment. You think you've been fighting for justice, but in reality, you've been pawns in a game that's been controlled for decades."

Jonas felt as if the world were tilting. His body felt heavy, as if the floor beneath him was collapsing. Every case he had worked on, every person he had defended, every moment he had spent in the courtroom now seemed insignificant compared to what he was hearing. What was the point of fighting for justice when the very concept of justice was being manipulated by powerful forces beyond his comprehension?

"You think you can stop us?" the man said, his voice dripping with disdain. "You think exposing us will change anything? The system has been built to withstand threats like you. You've already lost."

Jonas looked at Samira and Ethan, their faces grim but resolute. He couldn't let them give up now. The stakes were too high. This wasn't just about one case, one man. This was about the entire world—the very structure of reality itself.

He took a step forward. "We haven't lost. Not yet."

The man laughed, an eerie sound that echoed in the dimly lit room. "You think exposing us will change anything? That's adorable." He paused for a moment, staring at them with cold, calculating eyes. "But what if you're already part of the plan?"

Jonas's heart skipped a beat. "What do you mean?"

"We've been watching you," the man said, leaning back in his chair, a smug smile playing on his lips. "Every step you've taken, every question you've asked, has been anticipated. We know what you'll do next. We've been manipulating the entire system—*your* system, Jonas. You think you've been fighting to expose the truth? We've already rewritten your past. Your victories, your defeats, your career—every decision you've ever made is part of our design."

Jonas felt a wave of nausea sweep over him. The idea that his entire life could have been controlled, that his every action had been foreseen, was enough to make him question everything. Had he ever really been in control of his own choices?

"This can't be real," Ethan muttered, his voice low and filled with disbelief. "You're telling us we've all been part of your plan?"

The man didn't answer immediately. Instead, he stood up, his presence imposing as he walked toward them. "Yes," he said slowly, "you've been part of it all along. You were never meant to win. You were never meant to expose the truth. You were meant to play your parts in our game. And now, the endgame is upon you."

Jonas felt a cold sweat forming on the back of his neck. Every instinct in his body told him that this was it. The moment they had all been working towards. The moment they either succeeded or failed.

"Why tell us all this?" Samira asked, her voice steady despite the gravity of the situation.

"Because it's already over," the man replied, his voice filled with certainty. "You've come this far, but now you'll understand that all the pieces were never yours to control. The Revisionists control everything. We are the ones who shape history. And your fight is nothing more than a footnote in our grand design."

Jonas's mind raced, trying to grasp the enormity of what he was hearing. His hands shook as he balled them into fists, trying to maintain control. Samira and Ethan had been right—this wasn't just about exposing a corrupt system. It was about fighting against a force that controlled everything, a force that had the power to rewrite reality itself.

He took a deep breath, steeling himself for the inevitable.

"We're not done yet," Jonas said, his voice resolute. "We're going to expose you. We're going to show the world what you've done. And we're going to stop you."

The man looked at him with a cold, amused smile. "You're already too late, Jonas. It's over."

The room fell silent, the weight of his words hanging in the air. But Jonas didn't flinch. He couldn't afford to.

The fight for justice wasn't over. Not yet. And as long as there was breath in his body, he would keep fighting. Even if the rules had already been rewritten.

Eighteen

The Price of Truth

Jonas sat alone in his office, the silence pressing in on him like a suffocating weight. The walls, once familiar and comforting, now seemed to close in around him. His fingers tapped nervously against the cold surface of his desk as he stared at the glowing computer screen, his mind racing. He had spent years fighting for justice, defending the innocent, and trying to make a difference in a broken system. But now, with everything he had ever believed in crumbling before his eyes, Jonas was faced with a decision that could destroy him—or worse, erase him entirely.

He had always been a man of principle, committed to the rule of law and the idea of justice, no matter the cost. But now the very thing he had dedicated his life to seemed like an illusion. The Revisionists, this shadowy group that had manipulated the system for decades, had proven just how fragile the truth could be. They could erase not just people and evidence, but entire histories, entire lives. Nothing was sacred.

The past few weeks had felt like a nightmare—a nightmare he couldn't escape. Every step he took to expose the conspiracy, every case he dug into, every lead he followed, only seemed to bring him closer to an invisible wall. The more he uncovered, the more it seemed that he had no control over anything anymore. The people he had trusted had either turned their backs on him or, worse, were being manipulated themselves. And now, the life he had built—the career he had worked for— was slipping through his fingers like sand.

He glanced at the clock on the wall. It was late. Samira and Ethan had left hours ago, after they had gone through the final details of the information they had gathered. They had made progress, yes, but Jonas had sensed something different in their eyes. There was a weariness there, a sense of futility that hadn't been there before. Even they were beginning to question whether they could win this fight.

The phone on his desk rang, its shrill tone cutting through the stillness. Jonas stared at it, his hand hovering above the receiver. He knew who it was before he picked up.

"Jonas?" The voice on the other end was familiar, but there was an edge to it. It was Samira. "We need to talk."

His heart sank. "What's going on?"

"I've got something," she said, her voice low. "A lead, something big. But I'm not sure it's worth it."

Jonas could hear the uncertainty in her tone, and it sent a chill through him. Samira had always been the one with the answers, the one who kept her cool no matter what. But now, she was questioning everything.

"Samira, what is it?" Jonas pressed, his mind racing.

"It's about the Revisionists," she said slowly. "I've been digging deeper into their network. And there's something I found—something that connects them to a higher level of power, a level we haven't even touched yet."

Jonas leaned forward, his pulse quickening. "What are you saying? Are you telling me they're more powerful than we thought?"

"I don't know," Samira replied, her voice tense. "But I'm starting to think they might have been manipulating us all along. The things we've uncovered—they're all just part of a bigger picture."

Jonas's heart raced. The more he heard, the more his mind spun. It was becoming clear that the Revisionists had been controlling everything—*everything*—from the beginning. His own investigation, his own life, had been shaped by their unseen hand.

"I need to know what's going on," he said, his voice tight with urgency. "We can't let them win. We have to expose them."

Samira hesitated before responding. "That's just it, Jonas. What if exposing them means we disappear? What if it means the people we care about—*you*—vanish from history?"

Jonas closed his eyes. He had considered this possibility. He had been forced to, especially after the chilling warnings from the Revisionists themselves. But now, hearing it from Samira—someone who had always believed in the power of truth—he knew it was real.

He had always thought he knew what the price of truth was. He had spent his entire career fighting for justice, even when it was difficult, even when it meant losing everything. But now, he was faced with a choice that was more than just losing his career or his reputation. This was about losing his very existence. His memories, his identity, the life he had built—all of it could be wiped away if the Revisionists had their way.

"I can't let them do this," Jonas said, his voice shaking with a mixture of determination and fear. "I can't let them rewrite history, let them take away everything we've fought for."

Samira's silence stretched on, and Jonas could feel the weight of her words hanging in the air. Finally, she spoke again, her voice barely above a whisper.

"Then you'll have to choose, Jonas. Because once you expose them, there's no going back."

Jonas felt a lump form in his throat. The decision was his to make. The cost of truth had always been high, but now it felt more impossible than ever. He could expose the Revisionists, risk erasure from history itself, and try to stop them before they took even more lives. Or he could protect the people he loved—his colleagues, his family—and remain silent, allowing the system to continue its twisted manipulation of reality.

He thought of his family, his friends, the people who had stood by him all these years. If he exposed the truth, if he took down the Revisionists, what would happen to them? Would they, too, be erased from history? Would they remember him, or would they forget?

Jonas walked over to the window and stared out into the city. Eridale, the city he had lived in for years, now felt like a strange and distant place. The beautiful architecture, the grand buildings—it all felt like a façade, a mask hiding the rot beneath. How much of it was real? How much of it had been rewritten by the Revisionists? And how much of his own life had been manipulated without him even knowing?

He knew one thing for sure—he couldn't keep living like this. The fear, the doubt, the constant questioning of what was real— it was driving him mad. He had to make a choice. And that choice would define everything.

"I've made my decision," Jonas said, his voice steady.

Samira's voice was urgent. "What are you going to do?"

"I'm going to expose them," he said, his decision final. "No matter the cost."

There was a pause on the other end of the line, and Jonas could hear Samira's breath hitch. "Are you sure?"

Jonas stared at his reflection in the glass, his face pale and drawn. But he didn't hesitate.

"I'm sure."

As he hung up the phone, Jonas knew that his life, as he had known it, was over. There would be no turning back. But if he didn't act now, if he didn't take down the Revisionists, then everything would be lost—*everything*.

Nineteen

A World in Chaos

The city of Eridale had never felt more oppressive. The once pristine streets now seemed shrouded in a heavy fog of uncertainty. The weight of the conspiracy they were up against hung over Jonas, Samira, and Ethan like a storm cloud, darkening everything it touched. They had come so far, and yet, the closer they got to the truth, the more dangerous the world around them became.

The Revisionists were everywhere. They had eyes everywhere. And they were always watching.

Jonas could feel the walls closing in, the suffocating grip of the system they had uncovered tightening with each passing day. They had dug too deep. They had exposed too much. And now, the powers that be were prepared to do whatever it took to keep their secrets buried. As the hours slipped away, Jonas knew there was no more time to waste.

He was sitting in his office, the blinds drawn tight, his mind racing. Samira had gone to speak with a contact, trying to dig up more information on the elusive players behind the Revisionists. Ethan, ever the pragmatic one, had gone to investigate a potential lead in the heart of the city, a source who might have insight into the mastermind orchestrating this entire scheme.

Jonas was alone for now. But not for long.

The phone on his desk buzzed, its shrill tone breaking through the thick silence of the room. He grabbed it without hesitation, his pulse quickening as he heard Samira's voice crackle through the receiver.

"Jonas," she said, her voice sharp, "we have a problem."

Jonas sat upright, his heartbeat quickening. "What is it?"

"It's bad," Samira replied, her voice strained. "The Revisionists are moving faster than we thought. They're already starting to cover their tracks. People are disappearing, and the connections we've made—our evidence—it's all being erased. Someone is warning them, and they're getting closer to us."

Jonas leaned forward, his mind reeling. "What about Ethan? Did he make it to the lead?"

"He's not back yet," Samira said, a note of concern creeping into her tone. "I'm trying to reach him, but the lines are…well, they're not secure. We need to meet, Jonas. Now. We don't have much time."

The urgency in her voice sent a chill down his spine. He grabbed his coat, tossing a quick look at the office door before stepping into the hallway. Every move felt like a calculated risk now. He could sense the eyes of the Revisionists on him, even though he couldn't see them. The subtle shifts in the air, the small, seemingly inconsequential things—the crackle of the phone line, the strange feeling that he was being followed—told him that they were closing in.

The dimly lit alley behind the café smelled faintly of rain and exhaust. Jonas was waiting by the back door, his hand gripping the envelope with the information he had received hours earlier. Samira was late, which made his anxiety spike. Ethan was supposed to be with her, but he hadn't heard from him in hours. What was taking so long?

He shifted uncomfortably, his eyes scanning the empty street. There was no sign of her yet. Just as he began to wonder if something had gone wrong, he heard the familiar sound of footsteps behind him.

Samira rounded the corner, her eyes flicking nervously around the street. "We need to move," she said urgently, her voice low.

"What happened?" Jonas asked, instinctively stepping closer.

"We don't have much time," Samira replied, handing him a small piece of paper. "I think I've found out who's behind all of this."

Jonas glanced at the paper, his eyes narrowing. The name written on it—Julian West—was not unfamiliar. He'd heard whispers about him in hushed conversations, but it never felt like anything tangible. Until now. West was a name that didn't come up in most public records. He was a shadow, a man with no real identity, who moved between the corridors of power like smoke, always just out of reach.

"The head of the Revisionists," Jonas muttered.

"Yes," Samira replied, her gaze shifting. "And he's been involved in manipulating entire legal histories. The truth about what happened to Voryx Technologies—it's all connected. The AI systems they've developed have been used not just for technology, but for rewriting history itself. Julian West is at the center of it all."

Before Jonas could respond, there was a sudden noise from across the alley—a door creaked open. Jonas's instincts kicked in, and he motioned for Samira to get inside.

The Revisionists were here.

They moved swiftly, ducking into the dimly lit building behind the café. Jonas's mind raced. This was it. The moment of truth. If they didn't act fast, they would lose the one lead they had left.

Samira turned to Jonas, her face tense with determination. "We have to confront West. We have to expose everything before they erase us."

Jonas's throat tightened. "Do we even stand a chance?"

She hesitated, then nodded. "We don't have a choice."

Hours passed as they carefully made their way through the underbelly of the city. They could feel the weight of the surveillance in the air. Every step they took seemed to echo with the knowledge that their every move was being watched. Every time Jonas turned a corner, he half-expected to find himself staring down the barrel of a gun.

The alleys, once familiar and comforting in their anonymity, now felt like traps. Jonas's heart pounded in his chest, but Samira remained focused, guiding them forward.

Finally, they reached their destination—a nondescript door at the end of a narrow street. The kind of place where secrets were kept. Jonas's stomach churned with a growing sense of dread. This was it. The place where everything would either fall apart or be exposed for the world to see.

Samira knocked once, then twice, the sound reverberating

in the otherwise silent street. There was no answer at first, but then the door creaked open slowly.

"Samira Cross," a deep voice said, its owner stepping into the dim light. "I've been expecting you."

Jonas's heart skipped a beat as he saw the man standing before them—Julian West. The same name they had been chasing. The man who had been pulling the strings behind the scenes, manipulating not just legal systems but entire societies.

"Come in," West said smoothly, stepping aside. "Let's talk."

Inside the building, the air was thick with tension. The walls were lined with bookshelves filled with dusty legal texts, documents Jonas knew would be irrelevant within hours. The room smelled of old paper and secrets. A single lamp illuminated the room, casting long shadows on the walls.

West sat behind a desk, his eyes calm but calculating. He wasn't the kind of man who seemed like he had to try hard to command respect. He exuded authority simply by being there.

"You've come this far," West said, his tone almost mocking. "But you don't understand, do you? You think you're fighting for justice. But the truth is far more complicated than that."

Samira stepped forward, her face hardening. "What are you trying to do? What's your endgame?"

West smiled, a thin, sinister smile. "What do you think I'm doing? I'm rewriting history. I'm controlling the narrative. You, Jonas, Samira—your fight for justice? It's a futile endeavor. You're nothing but pawns in a game that's much larger than you. It's over."

Jonas clenched his fists, trying to keep his composure. "You're wrong. We're not just pawns. And we'll expose you. We'll take down your entire system."

West's smile widened. "You think you can expose me? Expose The Revisionists? You've already lost. You're already being rewritten. You just don't know it yet."

A chill ran down Jonas's spine. The air in the room grew heavier, as if the walls themselves were closing in.

"You can't rewrite everything, West," Samira said, her voice steady. "The truth always finds a way."

West's eyes gleamed with malice. "The truth is a luxury, Samira. And luxury is something you'll never have again."

Jonas's mind raced. The truth was slipping away. He could feel it. But he wasn't ready to give up. Not yet.

"We'll see about that," Jonas said, his voice unwavering.

The door slammed shut behind them, and the game was no longer a matter of just winning. It was about survival.

Twenty

The Vanishing Defense

The air in the room felt thick with tension, as if the very walls were closing in around Jonas, Samira, and Ethan. The weight of everything they had uncovered pressed down on them, heavier with each passing moment. They were standing in the heart of the storm now, with nowhere left to run.

The Revisionists had always been shadows, figures pulling strings from the darkness. But now, Jonas could see the full scope of their plan—an intricate web of power, control, and manipulation that stretched far beyond anything he could have imagined. The truth had been carefully hidden, buried deep within layers of deception, and now it was slowly, painfully, coming to light.

Jonas felt his stomach churn. The world around him seemed to shift, the air thickening, almost as if reality itself were starting to bend under the weight of their investigation. He turned to

Samira, who stood beside him, her face a mask of determination. Ethan, too, looked resolute, though the fatigue in his eyes was impossible to ignore.

They had uncovered everything—the connections between the powerful legal figures, the silent influence of Voryx Technologies, the manipulation of history, the rewriting of lives. But now, in this moment, everything came down to one final confrontation.

"This is it," Jonas said, his voice low but steady. "This is where it ends."

Samira nodded, her jaw tight. "We expose them now, or we lose everything."

They were standing in a secluded part of the building, hidden away from the prying eyes of the outside world. Their destination was the final meeting point with the last key players—the architects of The Revisionists' operation. It was here that Jonas would finally have the answers to all the questions that had plagued him.

The elevator doors slid open with a soft chime, and Jonas stepped inside, leading the way. The oppressive silence of the building seemed to follow them, wrapping around them like a blanket.

The tension was palpable as they descended to the final level—deeper into the bowels of the city, where the most secretive dealings were made. The walls were made of steel, and the corridor ahead seemed to stretch into infinity, a cold, impersonal hallway lit by harsh fluorescent lights. Everything about this place felt wrong—sterile, cold, and unnervingly quiet.

When they reached the door, Jonas paused, a sense of dread creeping up his spine. The sound of his own breath seemed loud in the silence, but there was no going back now. They had come too far.

He knocked once, twice, each strike a deliberate sound that echoed in the stillness.

The door swung open.

Inside, the room was dimly lit by a single overhead light, casting long shadows across the floor. A large desk stood at the far end, and behind it sat the man Jonas had been chasing for so long—Julian West. The mastermind. The leader of The Revisionists.

West's cold, calculating eyes met Jonas's, and for a moment, there was only silence.

"You're too late," West said, his voice low and smooth. "You've uncovered the truth, but it won't change anything."

Jonas felt a surge of anger, but he kept his voice steady. "It's not too late. Not yet. We're going to expose you. All of you."

West leaned back in his chair, a thin smile playing on his lips. "Expose us? You think you can stop something that's been in motion for decades? The system is already in place. Everything you've uncovered is already irrelevant. We've already erased it. Your lives—your histories—they'll all be rewritten."

Samira stepped forward, her voice unwavering. "The truth is more powerful than you think, West. You can erase people, but you can't erase the truth."

West chuckled softly. "You're naive. You think people will remember what you reveal? People will forget. They always forget. What we've done isn't just about erasing crimes. It's about controlling the narrative. About reshaping history to suit our needs. Your fight for justice is nothing more than a fleeting illusion."

Jonas's heart raced. The weight of West's words hung heavy in the air. They had come so far, but could they really stop this?

Could they expose The Revisionists before it was too late?

West stood from his chair and walked toward them, his footsteps slow and deliberate. He stopped just a few feet away, close enough for Jonas to feel the intensity of his gaze. "The people you're trying to protect—they're already erased. The system is ours now, Jonas. And you? You're just another pawn. A man of the law, but not even the law itself can save you now."

Jonas felt a chill run down his spine. Was it really over? Was this the end?

"No," Jonas said, his voice growing stronger. "We won't let you get away with this. We've already seen the cracks in your system. It's not as impenetrable as you think."

West's smile widened, but there was something darker in his eyes. "You think you can stop it? You think you can stop *us*? The wheels are in motion. There's no going back. You're already part of the game. Everyone is. Even you."

Jonas glanced at Samira and Ethan, who stood resolutely beside him. This wasn't over. Not yet.

A soft beep interrupted the tense silence. West's eyes flicked to a nearby screen, which flickered to life. The face of a man Jonas didn't recognize appeared, his image distorted by static. A voice crackled through the speaker.

"West," the voice said. "It's time. The final phase is about to begin."

West's expression hardened. "Yes. It's time."

He turned back to Jonas, his smile vanishing. "You've been a worthy adversary, Jonas. But now, you've outlived your usefulness. It's time to rewrite your part in this story."

Before Jonas could react, a blinding flash filled the room. The world around him seemed to warp, the floor beneath his feet shifting, and everything he had known, everything he had fought for, seemed to disappear.

The room twisted and distorted, and for a moment, Jonas couldn't tell if he was dreaming or awake. He reached out, grasping at the air, trying to steady himself. But the more he tried, the more everything seemed to slip from his grasp.

And then, the world went dark.

When Jonas regained consciousness, he was no longer in the room with West. He was lying on the cold, concrete floor of an unfamiliar place, the echoes of the earlier conversation still ringing in his ears.

"Jonas?"

He looked up to see Samira standing over him, her face a mixture of concern and determination.

"Samira," Jonas muttered, pushing himself into a sitting position. "What happened? Where are we?"

"We were attacked," Samira said, offering him a hand. "The Revisionists—they tried to erase us. But we're still here. We're not done yet."

Jonas blinked, still disoriented. "But West... we were just about to—"

"He's gone," Samira said, her voice grim. "But not for long. We have one last chance to stop them. And this time, we're not backing down."

Jonas nodded, the weight of their mission pressing down on him. He knew what they had to do now. It was time to stop running. It was time to confront The Revisionists once and for all.

But as they prepared to face their final battle, Jonas couldn't shake the thought that the battle wasn't just about exposing the truth—it was about reclaiming their own identities. About

proving that the truth could never be erased.
It was the only thing that mattered now.

Epilogue

The city lights flickered below, casting long shadows over Samira Cross as she sat in the dim light of her apartment, the only noise in the room the steady click of her keyboard. She had been staring at the screen for what felt like hours, the latest report still open, but she wasn't reading. Not really. Her thoughts were far from the article in front of her.

The trial. The disappearance of the evidence. The vanished cases. They all led to one undeniable conclusion: The system had been warped beyond recognition. What had begun as a simple investigation into a corrupt billionaire had spiraled into something much larger, something Samira couldn't fully comprehend. Every piece of truth she uncovered only made the darkness deeper, the questions more insistent.

Now, the world around her seemed to be unraveling. Her memories, once so solid, were shifting like sand, and the more she fought to hold onto them, the more they slipped away. Her name, once an undeniable part of her identity, was becoming nothing more than a shadow, a whisper that no one around her seemed to remember.

The phone on the table buzzed suddenly, snapping Samira

from her reverie. It was a text message from Jonas.

"I've found something. We need to meet. It's not over. Not by a long shot."

She picked up the phone, her fingers trembling slightly as she typed a reply.

"Where?"

Within moments, the address pinged on her screen. A place she knew well. It was a café where they'd met countless times in the past—before all of this had started. A small, quiet corner of the world where the noise of the city couldn't touch them. Where they could think without feeling like they were being watched.

Samira set the phone down, a cold shiver running down her spine. The weight of Jonas's words gnawed at her. *It's not over.* But what did that mean? What more could they be fighting for, when their very existence seemed to be on the brink of being erased?

She stood up from the desk and grabbed her coat, feeling the familiar weight of it settle over her shoulders. Her mind was a battlefield, a warzone of confusion, betrayal, and fear. She had fought to uncover the truth behind the disappearing cases, and now she was in the middle of something far worse—something far more dangerous. The shadowy tribunal, the rewriting of history, the erasure of innocent lives, and the cold realization that she was next.

As she stepped out into the cold night air, her breath visible in the chill, Samira tried to push the unease from her mind. She had made it this far. She had uncovered the truth. But every answer she found seemed to lead to even darker questions, and the closer she got, the more she realized the people pulling the strings weren't just altering criminal cases—they were rewriting reality itself.

The café was nearly empty when Samira arrived. She could see Jonas in the corner, his face lit by the glow of the lamplight, his eyes scanning the door as if expecting her. His expression darkened when he saw her, a mixture of relief and worry crossing his features.

"Samira," he greeted her with a nod, his voice low but firm. "You look like you've seen a ghost."

Samira smiled, though it felt forced. "I might have," she said, taking a seat across from him. "I can't keep track of what's real anymore."

Jonas leaned forward, his hands clasped together on the table. "I know the feeling." He glanced over his shoulder, then lowered his voice further. "Listen, I've been digging into something. I think I've found the next piece of the puzzle, but it's not what we thought."

Samira's heart skipped a beat. "What do you mean? What have you found?"

Jonas hesitated, then slid a file across the table. It wasn't the usual case notes or reports they had exchanged in the past. This file was different. The cover was dark, its contents unfamiliar.

"Look at this," Jonas said. "Reports are starting to emerge about a secret courtroom operating completely outside the law. Criminals who should've been convicted are suddenly vanishing—disappearing without a trace. It's like they never existed."

Samira opened the file, scanning the pages quickly. The information was sparse, but the implications were chilling. Criminals, once considered guilty, had mysteriously disappeared—never to be found. But worse still, the records of their crimes, the evidence, the testimonies—everything about them was wiped clean. There was no trace. No one could even remember their names.

Her mind raced. "A shadow court," she muttered. "What is this? Who's running it?"

Jonas shook his head. "That's the problem. We don't know. But there's something even worse. People aren't just vanishing— they're being erased from history. As if they were never there in the first place."

Samira's stomach tightened. She flipped through the pages, scanning every word. It wasn't just about criminals getting away with murder—it was about erasing entire lives, rewriting the very fabric of reality. History itself was being manipulated, as though someone had the power to decide who existed and who didn't.

"This is bigger than we thought," Samira said, her voice a whisper, a chill creeping up her spine. "It's not just about corrupt trials or erased cases. It's about controlling who we remember."

Jonas's expression was grim. "That's what I'm afraid of. And if we don't stop them, the truth will vanish—everyone who knows about it will vanish with it."

Samira's thoughts were clouded with a creeping terror. She had suspected something like this—an unseen force erasing pieces of reality. But to see it written down in black and white, to hear Jonas speak of it so openly, made it undeniable. They were facing something far beyond the scope of a single case or conspiracy. This was a war on truth itself.

Suddenly, Samira's phone buzzed, breaking her thoughts. She glanced at it quickly, her eyes scanning the screen. The message was short—too short—and from an unknown number.

"They know. They're watching. They won't stop."

Her fingers trembled as she set the phone down, her gaze meeting Jonas's.

"What is it?" Jonas asked, leaning forward.

Samira swallowed, trying to steady her breath. "Someone just sent me a message. They—whoever 'they' are—know we're onto them. And they're watching us."

Jonas's eyes narrowed. "We need to act fast. This thing is bigger than we imagined. If we don't expose them now, they'll rewrite everything."

As Samira looked down at the file on the table, a sudden realization hit her. She wasn't just fighting for justice anymore. She was fighting for her own existence. For her own memories. The deeper she dug, the more her life seemed to slip through her fingers. Her career—her family—her name were all fading, being erased, just like the people in the files Jonas had uncovered.

The truth was slipping away from her, but she wasn't ready to let go. She had come too far.

"We'll stop them," Samira said, her voice stronger now, a new determination rising within her. "But we'll need help. We need to find out who's behind this and expose them before they rewrite history completely."

Jonas nodded, his expression resolute. "We'll do it together."

And as they sat there, their minds racing with the weight of the task ahead, Samira knew one thing for certain: the truth had never been more dangerous. And whatever it took, she would expose it, no matter what was erased in the process.

The Vanishing Tribunal had begun, and there was no turning back.

www.ingramcontent.com/pod-product-compliance
Lightning Source LLC
Chambersburg PA
CBHW061320120726

48001CB00002B/607